AI On-Ramp

A Small Business Owner's First Thirty Days

By Jess Coburn

DISCLAIMER

The information contained in this book is for general informational purposes only. While we have made every effort to ensure the accuracy and completeness of the information presented, the rapidly evolving nature of artificial intelligence means that specific tools, capabilities, pricing, and best practices may change after publication.

The opinions expressed in this book are those of the author and do not necessarily reflect the views of any AI vendors, technology companies, or other third parties mentioned herein. Product names, logos, and brands are the property of their respective owners and are used for identification purposes only.

This book does not constitute legal, financial, or professional advice. Readers should consult with qualified professionals regarding their specific circumstances before making business decisions based on the information provided.

NO WARRANTY

The author and publisher make no representations or warranties with respect to the accuracy, applicability, or completeness of the contents of this book. The author and publisher specifically disclaim any implied warranties of merchantability or fitness for a particular purpose. Neither the author nor the publisher shall be liable for any loss of profit or any other commercial damages, including but not limited to special, incidental, consequential, or other damages.

THIRD-PARTY CONTENT

All product names, logos, services, and brands are the property of their respective owners. All company, product, and service names used in this book are for identification purposes only. Use of these names, logos, and brands does not imply endorsement. Pricing, features, and availability mentioned were accurate at the time of writing but are subject to change. Readers should verify current information directly with vendors.

First Edition: 2026

ISBN: 979-8-90514-135-5

CONTENTS

What's in here

BEFORE YOU START

How to Use This Book

This is a short book with a lot of instructions in it. Read it with the tool open.

Every chapter ends the same way, and the two sections at the end are the ones that matter most. **What to watch for** is where I tell you how the chapter goes wrong, which is usually more useful than the chapter. **Do this now** is a single task that takes a few minutes. If you do nothing else, do those.

The example exchanges are set off from the text, with your side of the conversation marked YOU and the tool's side marked IT on a tinted ground. They are real in shape and invented in detail: the numbers, names and clients are made up, and the responses are representative of what these tools produce rather than transcripts.

Part One gets you started, and it is the only part you have to read in order. Part Two is seven things you can do with it, and you can read those in any order you like. Part Three is four rules and takes eight minutes. Part Four is how to make it stick, and it is the part most people skip and shouldn't.

Two places name products and prices: Chapter 2 and the Appendix. Everything else in here is written to still be true in three years. When the two disagree with your screen, the screen is right.

There are three worksheets at the back. You will be sent to them from Chapters 13, 14 and 15.

Chapter 1 asks you to write a task on the inside cover of this book. That is not a figure of speech. Go find a pen.

⚠ **BEFORE YOU UPLOAD ANYTHING**

Until Chapter 12, use public, fictional, redacted, or nonconfidential material. Never enter passwords, credentials, identifying client or employee information, regulated or privileged data, or anything a contract prevents you from sharing. Work from copies, not originals. If you are unsure a document is safe to upload, do not upload it yet.

PART ONE

Just Try It

What the thing is, how to get one, your first ten minutes, and why it sometimes makes things up.

CHAPTER 1

What This Thing Actually Is

> *Think of AI as an incredibly well-read employee who has never worked at your company before.*

It's brilliant at patterns. It doesn't know your clients, your standards, or what matters in your world—yet. Your job is to guide it.

CHAPTER 1

What This Thing Actually Is

A partner at a small accounting firm told me last year that he'd already tried AI and it was garbage.

I asked what happened. He said he'd opened it up, asked for the section of the tax code covering a client's situation, and it handed him a citation. Confident. Formatted correctly. Section number and everything.

The section didn't exist.

He closed the tab and didn't open it again for eight months. I don't blame him. In his world, a made-up citation isn't a cute mistake. It's malpractice.

Here's the thing, though. He asked it to do the one thing it's the worst at, on his first try, and drew a conclusion about the whole tool. That's like hiring a sharp new associate, asking them on day one to recite a code section from memory, and firing them when they get it wrong.

This chapter exists to save you from that mistake. Once you understand what this thing is, its failures stop being surprising and start being predictable. Predictable failures are manageable. Surprising ones are what make people quit.

It is a guesser. AI just guesses ... Everything!

Strip away everything you've read and here's what's under the hood.

The AI engines are trained on an enormous amount of text: books, websites, manuals, transcripts, code, forum arguments, and product descriptions. Out of that training, they became extremely good at one basic operation: predicting what word is likely to come next. Technically, the unit is smaller than a word. For using the tool, "next word" is the useful mental model.

That's it. That's the whole machine.

Start typing "the balance sheet must" and it knows, from seeing that phrase in ten thousand places, that the next word is almost certainly "balance." Paste in a client's rambling voicemail and ask for a summary, and it guesses its way word by word through a summary, because it has seen a hundred thousand examples of long text followed by short accurate summaries.

If that sounds far too simple to be useful, you're having the correct reaction, and you're not alone. I had it too. The result is far more capable than that description makes it sound. When you make the system large enough and train it on enough text, prediction starts to look a great deal like thinking.

But it never stopped being a guesser. And that one fact explains everything it does well and everything it does badly.

Why this explains the fake citation

Ask it for a tax code section and, unless it clearly engages search or another reference tool, it may not look one up. It generates the most likely-looking answer, word by word, based on the patterns in citations it has seen.

Real citations have a pattern. A section number, a subsection, a familiar phrasing. So it produces something that matches the pattern perfectly. It looks right because looking right is the only job it has.

It wasn't lying to my friend. Lying requires knowing the truth. It was doing what it always does, which is producing the most plausible next words, and in that one case plausible and true came apart.

Hold onto that concept. Plausible and true came apart. Chapter 4 is all about when that happens and how to see it coming. For now, just know the failure isn't random. It has a shape.

The new hire

The comparison I keep coming back to, because it holds up better than any other, is a very sharp new hire.

Imagine someone joins your company on Monday. They've studied an enormous range of writing: textbooks, trade publications, manuals, and how-to guides across many industries. Their general knowledge is staggering. Hand them a badly written vendor contract and they'll often explain what it means in plain English faster than anyone on your staff.

But.

They've never worked at your company. They don't know your clients, your systems, your pricing, or the reason you stopped using that one vendor back in 2019. They weren't here.

They're also overly eager to help. Ask them anything and they may produce an answer immediately and confidently, because producing an answer is what they were hired to do. They sometimes say "I'm not sure," but you cannot rely on them to signal uncertainty. They can hand you something that sounds exactly like a correct answer.

That's what you're working with. Enormous general capability, no reliable knowledge of your specific business unless you provide or connect it, and no dependable instinct for admitting doubt.

Every good habit in this book comes from that one picture. You give it the context it doesn't have. You check the things it has no way of knowing. You use it for work where broad capability wins, and you stay skeptical on work where being here matters.

I want you to not forget the new hire concept. We'll come back to it.

What AI is actually good at

Since AI is a prediction system trained on an enormous range of text, it is excellent at many tasks that are fundamentally language problems.

Turning your rough notes into a clean client email. Reading forty pages of a lease and telling you what the renewal terms are. Explaining a complicated thing simply. Taking a messy list and organizing it. Drafting the first version of almost any document. Rewriting something you wrote in a hurry so it doesn't sound like you wrote it in a hurry.

Notice what those have in common. In every case, you already know whether the answer is right when you look at it. You read the summary of the lease and you can spot check it. You read the client email and you know if it sounds like you.

That's the sweet spot. It does the labor. You keep the judgment.

What AI is bad at, often really bad at

It's bad at anything where being confidently wrong is expensive and you can't easily tell.

Specific facts it would have to look up. Current information about anything, including your own business. Precise arithmetic done in its head, which sounds absurd for a computer but is true and gets its own section later. Anything that requires knowing your clients, your files, or your history.

And it's bad, in a way that catches people, at reliably telling you when it doesn't know. There is no calibrated confidence dial you can trust. A well-supported answer and an invented one can arrive in the same tone, in the same font, with the same apparent certainty.

WHAT TO WATCH FOR

The trap in this chapter is the opposite of my friend's trap.

He tried the hardest thing first, got burned, and quit. The more common trap runs the other direction. Someone uses it for a week, gets great results on writing tasks, and starts trusting it on everything. The confidence transfers. It drafted six good emails, so surely the number it just gave you is right.

The confidence shouldn't transfer. It's good at some things and bad at others, and it sounds exactly the same either way.

If you keep one sentence from this chapter, it's that one.

DO THIS NOW

Think of one task you did last week that was mostly words. A client email, a memo, a proposal paragraph, an answer to a question you've fielded fifty times. Write it down on the inside cover of this book.

That's the task you'll hand the bots in Chapter 3. Don't pick your hardest problem. Pick something boring you've done before, so you'll know right away whether the result is any good.

CHAPTER 2

Pick One and Sign Up

"

The good news is they're all quite good.
The better news is they're all free to try.

You don't need to pick the "best" one. Pick one and start. You can always try another later.

CHAPTER 2

Pick One and Sign Up

> Prices, plan names, and signup steps checked July 2026. These change faster than anything else in this book. Current version: jesscoburn.com/resources/.

So you're ready to start using AI. Well, I've watched more business owners get stuck here than at any other point in the process.

Not stuck on strategy. Not stuck on cost. Stuck on which one to pick. They read a comparison article, then another one, then a thread where two strangers argue about which is better at writing. Three weeks go by. They haven't typed a single word into any of them.

So let me shortcut the whole decision.

There are three main ones. They're all good. Pick any of them and start.

I'm not being glib. I use all three every week, and the honest answer is that for the work in this book, the difference between them is smaller than the difference between using one and using none. You're not choosing a spouse. You're opening a browser tab. If you pick wrong, which you probably won't, you can switch in about four minutes.

This chapter is the only place in this book where I name a product or quote a price, and that's on purpose. Everything else here will still be true in three years. This page won't be.

The three

ChatGPT, from a company called OpenAI. The one people have heard of. Broadest set of extra features, largest ecosystem, most third party guides written about it. If you want the option that the most people around you can help you with, this is it.

Claude, from a company called Anthropic. Tends to get picked by people whose work is heavy on writing and on reading long documents.

If your day involves contracts, reports, writing and drafting, a lot of professionals in your position land here.

Gemini, from Google. The differentiator is that it lives inside Gmail, Docs, and Sheets. If your firm already runs on Google Workspace, it shows up where you already are, which removes a real barrier.

If you're on Microsoft 365 rather than Google, there's a fourth option called Copilot that sits inside Word, Excel, and Outlook the same way. It's a reasonable choice for the same reason Gemini is.

That's the full landscape. Anyone who tells you it's more complicated than that is probably trying to sell you something.

How to choose in thirty seconds

Don't research this. Use whichever of these applies first.

- Your firm runs on Google Workspace? Use Gemini.
- Your firm runs on Microsoft 365 and you live in Excel? Use Copilot.
- Neither, and most of your day is documents and writing? Use Claude.
- Neither, and you want the most common option? Use ChatGPT.

Still torn between two? Flip a coin. I mean that. The cost of picking the slightly less ideal one is roughly zero. The cost of another three weeks of research is three weeks.

Free or paid

All of them have a usable free version. You can do real work on a free tier, although access and limits vary.

But you'll hit a wall. Free plans usually have lower usage limits and less access to the highest-capability models and tools. That can make a free tier a misleading way to form your first impression.

The paid personal plans generally sit at about twenty dollars a month. They raise limits and add features, but a paid personal subscription is not the same thing as a company-managed business workspace.

A business workspace may add company ownership, administration, offboarding, and different default data terms. It may also require multiple seats or an existing software subscription. Chapter 12 covers the decision, and the current comparison is at jesscoburn.com/resources/.

Start free for a few days. Pay within the first two weeks.

If you bill anything at all for your time, twenty dollars is the cost of about seven minutes of it. If this doesn't save you seven minutes a month you should stop reading and get your money back. It'll save you considerably more than that.

There's one more reason to pay that matters more than model quality, and I'm going to flag it here and explain it properly in Chapter 12. Consumer services may use conversations to improve their models, depending on the provider and your settings. Business workspaces generally give organizations stronger default data terms and administrative control. For anyone handling company or client information, that distinction matters more than small differences between models.

Signing up

Same for all of them, and it takes under five minutes.

- Go to the website. Not an app store, not a link someone texted you. Type the address into your browser. There are a startling number of fake apps with near identical names, and they exist to catch people doing exactly what you're doing right now.
- Click sign up. Use your work email, but remember that the email address alone does not turn a personal plan into a business workspace.
- Confirm the email.
- That's it. You're looking at a box.

The box is the whole interface. There's nothing else to learn. Everything in the rest of this book happens by typing into that box.

If the screen offers you a tour, take it. It's a minute and a half. If it offers you a template gallery, ignore it for now.

Get it on your phone too

Do this before you close the browser. Install the app on your phone and sign in with the same account.

The reason isn't convenience. The reason is that the habit forms in the gaps: the five minutes between meetings, the parking lot after a client visit, the moment you think of a question and then lose it. Having the same account on your phone makes it easier for the new habit to survive ordinary workdays.

WHAT TO WATCH FOR

Two things.

Don't sign up for all three. I know the instinct. You want to compare. What happens instead is you split your attention, none of them becomes familiar, and you end up with three accounts you use badly rather than one you use well. Familiarity is worth more than optimization here. Pick one. Give it a month.

Also, don't let your team sign up individually before you've read Chapter 12. They almost certainly already have, on their phones, with their personal email. That's not a crisis and Chapter 12 will tell you what to do about it. But don't formally send everyone off to create accounts yet. Get the one paragraph in Chapter 12 written first.

DO THIS NOW

Pick one using the thirty second rule above. Sign up. Install the phone app.

Then type this into the box, exactly as written, and read what comes back:

Explain what you are good at and what you are bad at, in plain English, for a small business owner who has never used you before. Be honest about the bad part.

That takes two minutes and it's a better introduction than anything I could write. Chapter 3 starts the moment after you've done the above task.

CHAPTER 3

Your First Ten Minutes

The first answer is the beginning of the conversation, not the end.

Great results rarely come from the first prompt.
They come from refinement.

CHAPTER 3

Your First Ten Minutes

Open the app. I'll wait.

I'm serious about this one. This chapter doesn't work if you read it on the couch and promise to try it later. Later doesn't come. There are three exercises here, they take about ten minutes together, and the whole point is that you do them while the page is open in front of you.

The exercises are ordered on purpose. The first shows you it can write. The second shows you it can read. The third shows you the thing almost everybody misses, and it's the one that decides whether this becomes part of your week or dies in a browser tab.

Go get the task you wrote on the inside cover in Chapter 1. We'll start with that.

Exercise one: make it write something

The mistake beginners make is typing a short vague request, getting a short vague answer, and concluding it isn't very good.

So let's do it wrong first, on purpose, so you can see the difference.

Type this:

YOU

Write an email to a client about a late payment.

Here's roughly what AI comes back with ...

IT

Subject: Friendly Reminder Regarding Outstanding Invoice

Dear [Client Name],

I hope this email finds you well. I am writing to follow up regarding invoice [Invoice Number], which was due on [Date] and remains outstanding.

We value our partnership greatly and understand that oversights happen. Please let us know if there are any issues we can assist with.

We would appreciate your prompt attention to this matter.

Best regards, [Your Name]

Perfectly fine and completely useless at the same time.

Useless because "I hope this email finds you well" is a phrase no human being has ever said out loud, and because you'd spend longer editing that than writing your own from scratch. This is the type of output (also called AI Slop) that makes people quit on day one, and they quit thinking the tool is weak when the real problem is that they told it nothing.

Now let's do it properly. Type this instead, with your own details swapped in:

YOU

I need an email to a client about a late invoice. Here's the situation. It's a landscaping company, about $8,400, forty-five days overdue. They've been a client for six years and have never once been late before. I like them. I think something is going on over there and I don't want to sour the relationship, but I also can't keep carrying it. Write it the way I'd actually talk. Short. No corporate filler.

IT

Subject: Checking in on invoice 4471

Hi Dave,

Invoice 4471 from May is still open, $8,400. Six years and this is the first time it's gone past due, which is why I'm reaching out instead of sending another statement.

Is everything alright over there? If it's a cash flow timing thing, tell me and we'll work something out. If it slipped through the cracks, no problem at all, just let me know when to expect it.

Either way I'd rather hear from you than keep wondering.

Talk soon, Ray

Read those two responses side by side.

The second one is usable. You might change a word here or there but it's still usable. That's the difference between four sentences of context and none, and it's probably the best thing you'll learn in this book.

The rule: it does what you tell it. Tell it the situation, the relationship, the tone, and the length. It can't read your mind, and it won't ask. It fills the gaps with generic filler because generic filler is the safest guess.

Now do this with your own task, the one from the inside cover. Just remember to give it a minimum of four sentences of context. Now go.

Exercise two: make it read something

This one tends to land hardest with people who bill by the hour, because the time savings aren't subtle.

Find a long document you've been avoiding. A lease, a vendor agreement, an insurance policy renewal, a forty-page report someone sent you. Something real that's sitting in your inbox making you feel slightly guilty.

You've got two ways to get it to the AI. Either drag the file straight into the box, which all of them now accept, or open it, select all, copy, and paste. Both options work. Dragging is easier.

Then, and this is the important part, ask a specific question instead of asking for a summary.

Here's the difference.

YOU

[drops in a 31 page equipment lease] Summarize this.

IT

This document is a commercial equipment lease agreement between the lessor and lessee covering the rental of industrial machinery. It outlines payment terms, maintenance responsibilities, insurance requirements, default provisions, and conditions for termination and renewal. The lease has a defined term with options for extension...

Well, it's Accurate. But it also tells you nothing you didn't already know from the title page.

Now ask it something you want to know.

YOU

[same 31 page lease] I'm about to sign this. Answer three things in plain English. First, what happens if I want out early and what does it cost me. Second, is there anything here that renews automatically, and if so what's the deadline to stop it. Third, list anything in this document that a reasonable person would consider unusual or aggressive compared to a standard equipment lease. Quote the actual language for anything you flag.

IT

Early termination. Section 11(c). You can terminate after month 24 with 90 days written notice, but you owe the remaining payments discounted at 4 percent, plus a "restoration fee" of $3,500. In practice, exiting in month 30 of a 60 month term costs you roughly $47,000.

Automatic renewal. Section 4(b), and this is the one I'd flag hardest. It renews for successive 12 month terms unless you give written notice between 120 and 90 days before expiry. Not "at least 90 days." There's a window, and notice given at 130 days is as invalid as notice given at 60. Your window opens roughly February 14, 2029.

Unusual provisions. Three:

- Section 9(a) puts maintenance entirely on you, including "any repair arising from ordinary wear," which is broader than standard and effectively means all repairs.
- Section 14 requires your insurance to name the lessor as loss payee and additional insured, and requires 30 days notice to them before any policy change. Your broker needs to see this.
- Section 18 waives your right to a jury trial and sets venue in Delaware. Standard in some industries, worth knowing you agreed to it.

[and it probably continued with two more sections]

That took about fifteen seconds. Finding the renewal window buried in section 4(b) yourself can take much longer, and it is easy to miss.

Notice what made the second attempt work. You told it what decision you were making. "I'm about to sign this" changes everything, because now it knows what matters and what doesn't.

Do this now with your own document. Ask it the question you actually care about.

Exercise three: talk back to it

Here's something almost everyone skips, and skipping it is why for most the first week with AI ends in utter disappointment.

It's a conversation, not a search box.

People type one thing, look at the answer, decide it's 70 percent right, and then either use it as is or give up. What they should do is what they'd do with a person. Say what's wrong and ask again.

Watch.

YOU

Draft a short note to my staff letting them know we are closing the office the Friday after Thanksgiving.

IT

Dear Team,

I am pleased to announce that our office will be closed on Friday, November 27th, in observance of the Thanksgiving holiday. This additional day off is a token of our appreciation for your continued hard work and dedication throughout the year.

We hope you enjoy the extended weekend with family and friends.

Warm regards,

Ok, that's Fine. But it doesn't sound like you, it's longer than it needs to be, and "token of our appreciation" is the kind of phrase that makes people wonder what the catch is.

Don't start over. Just say so.

YOU

Too formal and too long. We're eleven people, not a corporation. Cut it in half and make it sound like a normal person wrote it.

IT

Team,

We're closing the Friday after Thanksgiving, November 27th. Enjoy the long weekend.

One thing: if you're covering anything time sensitive that week, please make sure it's handed off before you leave Wednesday.

Ray

Ok, we're getting Better. And notice it added the handoff line on its own, which is the sort of thing that makes you go, huh, that's a good point.

Keep going.

YOU

Good. Drop the handoff line, I'll say that in person. And add one sentence at the end thanking them for the push on the year end filings.

IT

Team,

We're closing the Friday after Thanksgiving, November 27th. Enjoy the long weekend.

You earned it. The push to get the year end filings out the door was a real effort and I noticed.

Ray

Three exchanges. Under a minute. That's the note you send.

The habit to build: treat the first answer as a first draft, always. Never the answer. The first response is where the conversation starts, and the people who get real value out of this are the ones who push back two or three times without thinking twice about it.

You don't have to be polite about it. You also don't have to be rude. Just be clear. "Shorter." "Less formal." "You missed the point, the issue is X not Y." "Give me three versions." All of those work.

WHAT TO WATCH FOR

Two failure modes showed up in this first session, and both are worth naming before they happen to you.

The first is quitting after one bad answer. You'll get a bad answer today. Everyone does. Almost every time, the bad answer traces back to a vague request, and the fix is what we covered in exercise one and not a different tool.

The second is the opposite, and it's sneakier. The output is good, it's well organized, it's written with total confidence, and it's pleasant to read. That pleasantness is doing work on you. It's very easy to accept a well written wrong answer.

Exercise two is where this bites. It told you the renewal window is February 14, 2029. Did you check that against the lease? If you're about to sign something with $47,000 of exposure, you check. It's usually right a large majority of the time on that kind of task, and a large majority isn't the same as always.

Chapter 4 is entirely about this, and it's the most important chapter in Part One.

DO THIS NOW

If you skipped the exercises and read straight through, go back and do exercise three. Just that one. Ask it for something, then tell it what you didn't like, then tell it again.

That single loop is the difference between people who use this tool and people who tried it once.

CHAPTER 4

Why It Sometimes Makes Things Up

“

It doesn’t know what’s true.
It chooses what sounds right.

AI predicts the most likely next words based on what it has seen—not what is actually correct.

CHAPTER 4

Why It Sometimes Makes Things Up

In 2023 two lawyers in New York filed a brief with six court cases cited in it. The cases were well formatted, plausibly named, and attributed to real courts. None of them existed. The judge, understandably, had questions.

The story got told for two years as a cautionary tale about AI being unreliable. That's the wrong lesson, and the wrong lesson is dangerous, because it leaves you with nothing but a vague uneasiness.

The right lesson is that those lawyers asked it to do the one thing it's structurally bad at, took the answer at face value, and filed it. The failure wasn't random. It was predictable. And once you can predict it, you can work around it without much effort at all.

This is the most important chapter in Part One. Read it and, if you have to, read it again.

AI is optimizing for plausible

Back to Chapter 1. The machine guesses the next word. That's all it does.

Which means it isn't trying to be right. It's trying to be plausible. Those two goals overlap almost all the time, which is exactly why this is tricky. Most of the time the most plausible next words are also the true ones, and everything works beautifully.

Then you ask for something specific it does not have, and the two goals separate. Unless it searches or checks a source, it may still produce the most plausible-looking thing: a citation-shaped object, a statistic-shaped object, or a section-number-shaped object.

The industry calls this hallucination, which I've never liked, because it suggests something exotic and rare. It's neither. It's the machine doing what it always does, in a situation where doing that produces a wrong answer.

There is no tell

Here's the part that catches experienced, careful people.

When it's certain and correct, and when it has invented something whole, the output looks identical. Same confident tone. Same clean formatting. Same absence of hedging.

You've spent your whole career reading people. You know what it looks like when someone is guessing. The pause, the qualifier, someone's eyes going up and to the left. Every instinct you've developed for spotting uncertainty in a person is useless here, because those signals come from a person feeling uncertain, and there's nobody in there to feel it.

Remember the new hire from Chapter 1. Nothing about them announces which answers came from twenty years of reading and which one they made up on their walk to the office. That's not a character flaw. There's no mechanism in there for the difference to show.

You can't detect a fabrication by just reading it. You detect it by knowing what kinds of questions produce them.

The four danger zones

Almost every fabrication falls into one of these.

1. Specific facts it would have to look up. Citations, statute numbers, page references, publication dates, who said what and when. The more precise and checkable the fact, the more suspicious you should be, which is the exact opposite of the instinct precision normally triggers.
2. Anything recent. When it answers from model memory, its knowledge may be stale even if the product also has a search feature. Prices, product versions, who runs what company, and what the rules are now should trigger a search and a source check.
3. Anything about your business. It doesn't know your clients, your revenue, your systems, or your history. Ask it something specific

about your firm without telling it anything and it'll build you a plausible fiction. This one's rare in practice because most people wouldn't think to ask, but it catches people in longer conversations where it starts filling in gaps.

4. Arithmetic. Which deserves its own section, because it's the one that surprises everybody.

Why on Earth is computer bad at math

I know. It sounds like a joke.

But remember what the thing is. It isn't a calculator with a chat interface bolted on. It's a language machine that learned by reading. When you ask it to add a column of numbers, it isn't calculating. It's guessing what the answer looks like, based on having seen enormous quantities of arithmetic written down.

For small familiar sums it gets it right, because it has effectively memorized them. For a column of thirty four figures with cents, it produces a number that has the right shape and the right magnitude and is off by a bit.

The number looks completely reasonable. That's the problem. A wildly wrong number you'd catch. One that's off by $340 on a $70,000 total slips through.

The good news is there's a fix, and it's easy. Modern versions can write and run code to do the arithmetic instead of guessing at it. Just tell it to: "Calculate this using code, don't do it in your head." Code makes the calculation reproducible and easier to audit. It does not guarantee that the tool understood the right rows, columns, or business rule. Some versions invoke code automatically; if yours does, you'll usually see a note that a calculation ran.

If you take nothing else from this chapter, take that. Any time real numbers matter, say "use code to calculate this," then inspect the inputs and logic. Chapter 8 goes deeper.

The looking things up problem, partly solved

One honest update, because the picture has changed and it'd be misleading to leave it out.

These tools can now search the web. When they do, they're no longer guessing from memory. They're reading a real page and telling you what it says, usually with a link. That fixes a large share of the recent information problem and a good share of the fabricated fact problem.

Two cautions.

They don't always search when they should. If a question smells like it needs current information, tell it to look it up rather than assuming it will.

And searching moves the problem rather than removing it. Now it's faithfully reporting what a web page said, and web pages are wrong all the time. If it hands you a link, the link isn't decoration. It's there for you to click.

The rule that replaces all of this

You don't need to memorize four danger zones. You need one question, and you can apply it in about two seconds before you use any output.

Would I know if this were wrong?

That's it. That's the whole thing.

You would know. Read the client email it drafted and you know instantly whether it sounds like you. Read the lease summary and you can check section 4(b) yourself in half a minute. Read the explanation of a concept you already understand and you'd spot the error. In all of these cases, use it freely and stop worrying.

After all, you wouldn't know. A citation you've never read. A statistic you have no independent sense of. A total you didn't calculate. A claim about a regulation you aren't fluent in. In those cases, you have two choices and only two: verify it, or don't use it.

The trap is the middle ground, where it sounds authoritative on something you can't check and you use it anyway because it sounded so certain. That's where the New York lawyers ended up. Not through carelessness exactly. Through the reasonable human habit of trusting confident prose.

WHAT TO WATCH FOR

The danger isn't Chapter 4 week. Chapter 4 week you're appropriately careful.

The danger is month three. By then it has been right hundreds of times in a row. It has drafted your emails, summarized your documents, explained things clearly, saved you real hours. Trust has been earned honestly.

And then one day you ask it something in one of the four danger zones, and you've stopped asking yourself whether you'd know if this were wrong, because asking felt paranoid after all that.

That two second check has to survive the trust. Write it on a sticky note if you have to. Would I know if this were wrong?

DO THIS NOW

Take something you know cold. Your industry's licensing requirements, a rule you apply every week, the specifics of a regulation you could recite in your sleep.

Ask it a detailed question about that thing. Then grade the answer like you're marking an exam.

You aren't doing this to catch it. You're doing this to calibrate it. You need one direct experience of seeing where the edges are on a topic where you're the expert, so you know what the edges feel like on topics where you aren't.

Almost everyone who does this comes away with the same two reactions, in this order: it's better than I expected, and it was wrong about one thing and I never would have known.

Both reactions are correct. Hold on to both.

PART TWO

Real Work

Seven jobs it does well. Read them in any order.

CHAPTER 5

Writing the Things You Write Every Week

"

Good writing isn't about finding the right words. It's about making your ideas easy to understand.

AI helps you turn rough thoughts into clear, professional communication—so you can focus on what matters most.

CHAPTER 5

Writing the Things You Write Every Week

There's a letter you've been meaning to write for about five months.

I don't know which one it is. Fee increase, probably. Or the one telling a long-standing client that you can't keep absorbing scope. Or the job posting for the role you've needed to fill since spring. Whatever it is, it isn't hard because it's a complicated task. It's hard because it's awkward, and awkward writing has a way of sliding to the bottom of the list every single day.

That letter is where this chapter starts, because the first real win with this tool is almost never a task you were doing efficiently. It's a task you weren't doing at all.

The trade is simple: it drafts, you edit. That's the whole arrangement. It's much faster than you at producing a first version and much worse than you at knowing what's right. Staring at a blank page is the expensive part of writing. AI removes the blank page.

Three examples. Do them in order.

Example one: the letter you have been avoiding

The fee increase. Everyone's favorite message to write or receive.

The reason this one stalls isn't that you don't know what to say. It's that you have to hold three things at once: be direct enough to be clear, warm enough not to damage a relationship you value, and firm enough that it doesn't read as an opening offer. Holding all three while typing is hard, so you close the window and do it tomorrow.

Give it all three and let it hold them.

YOU

I need to write to about thirty of my clients telling them my monthly fee is going up. Context: I haven't raised prices in four years. My costs are up substantially, mostly wages, and I'm currently doing more for most of them than what we originally scoped. The increase is 12 percent, effective January 1. These are good long term relationships and I don't want this to feel like a shakedown. I'm also not looking to negotiate. Write it once, in a way I can personalize per client. Be direct. Don't apologize for it.

IT

Subject: A change to your monthly fee, effective January 1

Hi [Name],

I am writing to let you know that your monthly fee is increasing by 12 percent starting January 1. For you that moves it from [current] to [new].

This is the first increase in four years. In that time our wage costs have risen considerably, and the work we do for you has grown well beyond what we originally scoped, which I have been happy to absorb up to a point. That point has arrived.

I wanted you to hear it directly from me, with plenty of notice, rather than finding it on an invoice in January.

Nothing else changes. Same team, same work, same responsiveness.

If you want to talk it through, call me. I am always glad to hear from you.

[Signature]

Read that carefully, because a few decisions in it are worth noticing.

It gave the number in the first sentence rather than burying it in paragraph three. It explained the reason in two sentences without pleading. It didn't say sorry. And "if you want to talk it through, call me" is warm without inviting a negotiation, which is a fine distinction that it got right on the first pass.

Would you send it exactly as written? Probably not. You'd change three or four words to sound like you. But you're now editing, and editing takes four minutes. The letter that's been sitting on your list since March is done before your coffee gets cold.

Push it further. Two follow ups that are worth making a habit.

YOU

Give me a shorter version for the six clients I know well enough to text.

YOU

Now tell me honestly what the two most likely pushbacks are and how you'd answer each one.

That second one is the sleeper. It'll hand you the objections before you get them, which means you aren't thinking on your feet when the first call comes in.

Example two: feed it your mess

Job postings are the clearest illustration of a habit worth building, which is: don't compose a request, dump your raw material.

I'm going to keep this one general, because the lesson has nothing to do with what business you're in.

Most people, faced with writing a job ad, try to write a tidy description of what they want and then hand over the tidy version. That's backwards. You're doing the hard work yourself and handing over the easy part.

Give it the mess instead.

YOU

I need a job posting. I'm going to give you my actual notes, not a clean description. Sort it out.

Notes: need a treatment coordinator. 2-3 yrs in a practice, not fresh out of school, I don't have time to train from zero. Must be able to sit down with a patient and talk about money without me in the room, this is the thing that keeps failing. Small practice, 6 of us, we are not a chain, nobody is on commission and I am not going there. Salary 52-62 depending. Four day week, we're closed Fridays, that is not changing. Dentrix and insurance verification obviously. The last two people I hired were lovely and could not handle a patient asking why the crown wasn't covered. That is honestly the whole job. Also 401k, decent health, two weeks off to start.

IT

Treatment Coordinator Wellington, FL. Four day week, Monday through Thursday. $52,000 to $62,000.

We are a six person practice and we need someone who can talk to patients about money.

That is not a soft skill line at the bottom of this posting. It is the job. Patients say yes to treatment and then get to the front desk and find out what their plan actually covers, and that conversation decides whether they go ahead or quietly disappear. It needs a person who can explain a benefits breakdown clearly, sit with someone while it lands, and not go find the dentist every time. If that describes you, keep reading. If it does not, this role will make you miserable.

What you will do

- Present treatment plans and financial arrangements to patients
- Verify benefits and know what each plan will and will not cover before the conversation, not during it
- Handle the "why isn't this covered" call yourself
- Keep the schedule full, which mostly means following up on treatment people already accepted

What we need

- Two to three years in a dental practice. We are not set up to train someone from zero.
- Dentrix and real comfort with insurance verification
- The confidence to be the answer rather than the messenger

What we offer

- $52,000 to $62,000 depending on experience - 401k, solid health coverage, two weeks paid time off from day one
- Four day week. We close Fridays and we are not quietly going to start opening them.
- No commission, no production targets, no upselling

How to apply Send a resume and tell us about a time a patient was upset about a bill and you fixed it.

The point isn't that this is a great posting, although it's a decent one. The point is what happened structurally.

You wrote for two minutes, badly, in fragments, the way you'd talk. It found the thing you said twice, which was that the money conversation is what keeps breaking, and it made that the headline instead of burying it in a bullet. It turned "nobody is on commission and I am not going there" into a benefit rather than a shrug. It converted "that is honestly the whole job" into an actual opening paragraph.

Swap the details and it's the same exercise for a roofer hiring an estimator or a shop hiring a lead machinist. The mess is the input. Sorting it is the job you're handing over.

Dumping your mess is a skill and it's the opposite of what people expect. You aren't supposed to clean up before you hand it over. The cleanup is the part it's good at.

And if you hate typing, don't type. Every one of these has a microphone button. Press it and talk for two minutes the way you'd explain it to someone in your truck. It transcribes as you go and handles the ums and the doubling back without being asked. For anyone who thinks faster than they type, and that's pretty much every business owner I know, this is the difference between using this thing and meaning to get around to it one day.

Example three: the fiftieth time

Now the one with the most compounding value, and the one that leads into our Chapter 11.

Every business has explanations you've written fifty times. Why we need the documents by the fifteenth. What the engagement letter covers. Why the estimate went up. Why we can't do the thing the client saw a competitor do (or, more likely, just say they do).

You've written each of these dozens of times, slightly differently, and never quite as well as the best version you ever managed.

Watch what happens when you stop rewriting and start building.

YOU

Every year I explain to clients why their extension is not a payment extension. They think filing an extension means they don't have to pay yet. Write me the explanation.

IT

An extension gives you more time to file your return. It does not give you more time to pay what you owe.

If you expect to owe, that payment is still due on the original deadline. Filing an extension without paying means interest and penalties start accruing from that date, even though your return is not due yet.

The practical version: estimate what you will owe, pay it by the original deadline, then take the extra months to get the paperwork right.

It's Good. It's Correct. But it's also slightly cold.

YOU

That's right but it reads like a form letter and it'll make people feel dumb for asking. They ask this because it doesn't make sense on the surface. Rewrite it so it starts by agreeing that it's confusing. And add one concrete number example, because that's what makes it land.

IT

I get this question every year and it is a fair one, because honestly the name is misleading.

An extension extends your time to file. It does not extend your time to pay. Those are two separate deadlines that happen to share a date, and nothing about the extension changes the second one.

Here is what that looks like in practice. Say you owe $9,000 and you file an extension in April. Your return is not due until October, which is fine. But that $9,000 was due in April. By October you are looking at interest plus a monthly penalty on the unpaid balance, which on that amount runs a few hundred dollars.

So the move is: estimate what you owe, pay it in April even if the return is nowhere near ready, then use the extra months to get it right without the meter running.

If you are not sure what to estimate, call me. A rough number paid on time beats a perfect number paid late.

That's better than what you'd have written on the fly, and considerably better than the version you sent in a hurry last April.

Here's the move that changes everything. Don't just use it. Save it.

Every one of these tools lets you keep a set of standing instructions or saved documents. Put your voice and your firm's specifics in there once. Then next April you don't rewrite this explanation. You ask for it, and it comes back already sounding like you.

That'll come Chapter 11, and it's the difference between a tool you use and a tool that works the way your firm works. For now, start a document called "explanations" and paste the good ones in as you make them. In six months that file is worth real money.

WHAT TO WATCH FOR

It'll make you sound better than you are, and that isn't always what you want. The drafts come back polished. If your normal emails are three blunt lines, a smooth four paragraph reply will read as strange to people who know you. Tell it to match how you actually write, and be specific. "Short. No greeting. I sign off with just my first initial."

Never send the first draft on anything that matters. Not because it'll be wrong. Because it'll be generic in a way you stop noticing. After a month of using it you develop a blind spot for the smooth version. Read it once with fresh eyes and ask whether a human being you respect wrote it.

Watch for the tells. Certain phrases recur and people are getting good at spotting them. "I hope this email finds you well." "Delve." "It is worth noting that." "In today's fast paced business environment." Cut them on sight. If a client thinks a machine wrote your fee increase letter, you've created a problem that didn't exist before. Oh, and never, ever allow it to include an "em dash." It's that extra-long dash — the one that screams AI wrote this. Did you catch it?

DO THIS NOW

Write down the awkward letter you've been avoiding. The actual one.

Give it four sentences of context and the three things you're trying to balance. Then edit what comes back and send it today.

Not this week. Today. That letter has been on your list long enough, and the whole argument of this chapter is that the reason it sat there was never the writing.

CHAPTER 6

Reading What You Don't Have Time to Read

Information is everywhere.
Understanding is the bottleneck.

AI helps you cut through the noise, surface what matters, and move from overwhelmed to informed.

CHAPTER 6

Reading What You Don't Have Time to Read

Somewhere in your email is a folder called "review this." Or there's no folder and there's just a low grade hum of documents you've received, opened, scrolled two pages into, and left.

The renewal packet. The sixty survey responses your office manager collected in March. The revised agreement with the changes supposedly marked. The email chain with forty two different replies that you were added to around message thirty eight.

None of these are hard. All of them are long. And long is the thing that's been quietly rationing your attention for your entire professional career.

Chapter 3 gave you the basic move, which is to drop a document in and ask a specific question instead of asking for a summary. This chapter goes past that, because reading comes in shapes, and each shape has its own move.

Four shapes. The pile, the redline, the thread, and the shelf.

Shape one: the pile

This is the one that's impossible by hand, which is why most people never do it.

You have sixty responses to a client survey. Or a hundred and forty reviews. Or eighteen exit interviews collected over three years. Individually each one takes forty seconds to read. Collectively they contain a pattern that no single one of them contains and finding that pattern means holding all sixty in your head at once, which nobody can do.

Here's my first attempt, which is the one you'll probably make too.

YOU

[pastes 60 client survey responses] Summarize the key themes in these client survey responses.

IT

Overall client sentiment is positive, with most respondents expressing satisfaction with the quality of service received. Several themes emerged:

Communication. Many clients commented on communication, with some praising responsiveness and others noting room for improvement.

Value. Respondents generally felt the services provided good value, though a minority raised concerns about pricing.

Technology. Some clients mentioned the client portal, with mixed feedback regarding ease of use.

Overall, clients appreciate the firm's expertise while identifying opportunities for enhanced proactive communication.

That's what a summary gets you. Read it again and notice that every sentence contains a hedge. Many. Some. Several. A minority. Generally.

You cannot do anything with that. You can't take it to a partner meeting, you can't decide anything from it, and worst of all you can't tell whether it's true, because there isn't a single checkable fact in the whole thing. It's a summary of the shape of your survey rather than its contents.

The fix is to ban the hedges and demand the receipts.

YOU

[same 60 responses] Don't summarize them. I want to know what people are actually saying when you look at all of them together. Specifically: what comes up more than three times, what's the single most common complaint, and is there anything here that surprised you. Count things. No "some" or "many," give me numbers. Quote real responses so I can see I'm not just getting your interpretation.

IT

What comes up repeatedly

Responsiveness, 22 mentions. This dominates, and it splits in an interesting way. Fourteen are positive and eight are negative, and the negative ones cluster almost entirely in February through April. Two people used the word "vanish."

Proactivity, 17 mentions, and almost all negative. This is your real finding. The complaint is not that you do bad work. It is that clients hear from you when they contact you and rarely otherwise. Representative:

- "They are great when I call. I just wish I did not always have to call."
- "I found out about the deduction change from my brother in law."
- "Reactive, not a partner."

Pricing, 9 mentions. Fewer than you might expect, and six of the nine are people saying you are worth it. Only three complain about cost.

Technology, 11 mentions. Mostly the portal. Six people find it confusing. Two said they email documents instead because the portal is easier to avoid than to learn.

Most common single complaint

Not being told about things that affect them until they ask. Seventeen responses. This is nearly double the next item.

What surprised me

Three separate people mentioned a specific staff member by name, positively and unprompted, which is unusual in survey data. Two said some version of "as long as she is there I am staying." That is a retention fact about your firm sitting in a customer satisfaction survey.

Also worth noting: nobody at all mentioned accuracy or errors. For an accounting firm that is a meaningful silence.

Same sixty responses. Same tool. Same two minutes. The difference is entirely in what you asked for.

Three instructions did that work. "Don't summarize." "Count things, no some or many." And "quote real responses so I can see I'm not just getting your interpretation."

That last one matters most, and not for the reason you'd think. It isn't about trust. It's about verification. With the quotes in hand you can spot check five of them against the source in two minutes and know whether to believe the other fifty five. Without them you have a smooth paragraph and no way in.

Make that a reflex. Any time AI is telling you what a pile of documents says, make it show its work.

Shape two: the redline

Someone sends back a revised agreement and says they made a few small changes. You now have two documents and a suspicion.

Comparing them by hand is miserable, which is why people mostly don't. They skim, they see nothing alarming, they sign. The change that matters is on page nineteen in a subsection about notice periods.

YOU

I'm giving you two versions of the same agreement. The first is what I sent. The second is what came back from their lawyer, who described the changes as minor cleanup. Tell me every substantive change. Ignore formatting, typos, and anything that doesn't change what either party has to do. For each one, tell me who it favors and whether I should care.

IT

Eleven changes. Six are genuinely cleanup. Five are not. Here are the five.

1. Section 5.2, payment terms. Net 30 became net 45. Favors them. This is the one with the clearest dollar cost to you.

2. Section 8.1, limitation of liability. Their cap went from "fees paid in the preceding twelve months" to "fees paid in the preceding three months." Favors them substantially. On your contract value that drops their maximum exposure by roughly three quarters.

3. Section 12.4, termination notice. You went from 30 days to 90 days notice to terminate. Their notice period stayed at 30. Favors them, and it is now asymmetric, which it was not before.

4. Section 14, indemnification. One word. "Shall indemnify" became "shall use commercially reasonable efforts to indemnify." That sounds like nothing and is not nothing. It converts a firm obligation into a soft one.

5. Section 3.1, scope. Added "or such other services as the parties may agree in writing." Neutral to mildly helpful. Probably genuine cleanup.

My read: items 2, 3, and 4 are not cleanup. They moved risk from them to you in three separate places, each individually small enough to pass a skim. Item 4 in particular is the kind of change that is easy to miss and expensive to discover later.

Whether or not you accept its judgment, you now know where to look. Fifteen minutes with your attorney instead of ninety, and you walk in knowing the three sections that matter.

Shape three: the thread

You get added to an email chain on message thirty eight. There's a meeting in twenty minutes.

YOU

[pastes the whole chain] I just got added to this and I have a meeting about it shortly. Catch me up. What's the actual disagreement, who wants what, what's already been decided so I don't reopen it, and what's currently waiting on someone.

IT

The disagreement. Whether the phase two work starts before the phase one punch list is closed out. That is it. Everything else is downstream of that one question.

Positions. Marcus wants to start phase two now, because his crew is available in September and will not be in November. Diane wants phase one signed off first, because she was the one who ate the cost last time this happened. Neither has said this directly. They have been arguing about the schedule.

Already settled, do not reopen. The budget number was agreed on in message 14. The vendor selection was closed in message 22. Both were contentious and both are done.

Currently waiting. Message 36, Diane asked for the punch list in writing. Nobody has sent it. That is the actual blocker and it has been sitting for nine days.

The last line is the most useful one. Meetings like this usually run forty minutes before someone works out that everyone's waiting for a document nobody has produced.

Shape four: the shelf

The first three shapes are things you read once and put down. The fourth is different, and it's the one most owners don't know exists.

You have a shelf. Not a literal one. It's the set of documents you keep going back to, month after month, and never quite know cold. Your three insurance policies. The employee handbook nobody has read since 2021 or probably updated since it was first generated. The standards manual for your trade. Nine years of engagement letters. The four vendor contracts currently in force.

Dropping those into a chat window one at a time works, and it's what Chapters 3 and 6 have had you doing. But you're re-uploading the same documents every time and starting from nothing every time.

There's a separate kind of tool for this and it's worth knowing about. You load your documents in once, they stay there, and you ask questions across all of them whenever you want.

The thing that makes it different is a restriction rather than a feature. It answers only from the documents you gave it. It won't reach for general knowledge, it won't fill a gap with something plausible, and it tells you which file each part of the answer came from.

YOU

Across all four vendor contracts, which ones auto-renew and what notice do I have to give?

IT

Three of the four auto-renew.

Ellison Supply [Ellison_Agreement_2024.pdf, section 4.2] renews for 12 month terms. Written notice required 60 days before the anniversary date of March 3.

Datapoint Systems [Datapoint_MSA.pdf, section 9] renews for 24 month terms, which is the one I would look at first, and requires 90 days notice. There is no mechanism in this document to convert it to a shorter term.

Coastal Facilities [Coastal_Service_Agreement.pdf, section 11(b)] renews month to month after the initial term ends. 30 days notice, no window.

Brennan Freight [Brennan_Terms_Signed.pdf] has a fixed end date of December 31 with no renewal language I can find. Confirm this one yourself, because I am telling you something is absent rather than present.

Read the last line again. It flagged the limit of its own answer, and it flagged the exact thing this chapter's "what to watch for" section is about to warn you against.

Why this matters after Chapter 4. The failure that made you nervous, the confident invented citation, is structurally much harder here. It's quoting your files and naming them. You can open the document and check in ten seconds. It can still misread something. It can't invent a contract you don't have.

For a shelf you consult a few times a month, this is worth the twenty minutes it takes to set up. Everything else in this book stays in the box.

WHAT TO WATCH FOR

Long documents can lose the middle. These tools handle enormous amounts of text now, far more than a few years ago, but attention across a very long document isn't perfectly even. Details buried in the middle of a two hundred page filing are the most likely things to get skipped.

Two defenses. Ask it to quote the actual language for anything it flags, which forces it back to the source. And if the document is huge, feed it in sections rather than all at once.

Absence is unreliable. If it tells you the contract contains a bad clause, and quotes it, believe it. If it tells you the contract contains no such clause, that's much weaker evidence. Confirming something is present is easier than confirming nothing is present, for a machine and for a person. Never rely on it to prove a negative on anything expensive.

This holds for the shelf too, and it's why the Brennan Freight line in that example was worded the way it was. A tool that quotes your own files is on solid ground when it says here it is. It's on exactly the same shaky ground as everything else when it says there isn't one.

A shelf is only as good as what you put on it. Two practical notes, and the appendix has the current details. Some locked or copy-protected files refuse to load and you'll get an error that doesn't explain itself. And a web address usually pulls in the text of a page only, so if what you need is a scan or an image, save it as a document and upload that instead.

It won't tell you what you didn't ask. In the redline example it found five substantive changes because it was asked for substantive changes. Ask a narrow question and you get a narrow answer with no warning that you missed the important thing. When you're in unfamiliar territory, add "and tell me anything else I should be asking about" to the end of the request. It's a small habit that has saved me more than once.

DO THIS NOW

Go find the longest thing in your inbox that you've opened and not read.

Drop it in. Then ask it the question you'd ask a trusted colleague who had read it for you, phrased exactly the way you'd phrase it out loud.

Not "summarize this." Something like "am I going to regret signing this" or "what's the one thing in here that's going to cause a problem." Talk to it the way you'd talk to the colleague.

CHAPTER 7

Explaining Complicated Things Simply

If you can't explain it simply,
you don't understand it well enough.

AI helps you translate complexity into clarity—so your team, your clients, and you can actually take action.

CHAPTER 7

Explaining Complicated Things Simply

The curse of knowing your job well is that you forget what it was like not to.

You've been doing this for twenty years. The thing you're explaining to a client isn't complicated to you. It's Tuesday. So you explain it the way it sits in your head, which is compressed, full of shorthand, and roughly four levels above where they are.

They nod. They say thanks. They call back in three weeks with the same question phrased differently, and you realize the first explanation never landed at all.

Chapter 6 was about it reading things for you. This chapter runs the other direction. You're the expert here. It knows nothing about your clients or your work that you don't tell it. What it's extraordinarily good at is taking something true and complicated and finding the version of it that a specific person can absorb.

That's a translation job, and translation is the thing it does best.

Example one: down a level

The most common version. You wrote the correct answer. It's too dense.

Here's the request most people make first.

YOU

A client asked why her quarterly estimated payment went up when her income didn't. Explain it simply.

IT

Great question! Taxes can definitely be confusing, so let's break it down step by step.

Think of your estimated payments like a monthly subscription for your taxes. Sometimes the amount changes even when your income stays the same. This can happen for a few reasons:

- Changes in withholding. If less tax is being taken out somewhere else, more has to be paid here.
- Safe harbor calculations. The IRS allows several methods for calculating estimated payments, and the applicable method may have changed.
- Prior year adjustments. Your prior year return can affect your current year requirement.

The good news is this doesn't necessarily mean you owe more overall. Your accountant can walk you through the specifics of your situation. Hope this helps clear things up.

Two separate problems there, and they're the two you'll see over and over.

The first is that it doesn't know why her payment went up, so it listed every reason a payment might go up. That's a textbook, not an answer. The second is the tone. "Great question," an exclamation point, and a subscription metaphor that doesn't fit. A woman who runs a business is being handed a pamphlet.

Both problems have the same cause. You asked it a question when it needed a briefing.

YOU

A client asked why her quarterly estimated payment went up when her income did not. The real reason is that last year's payments were based on the prior year safe harbor, her withholding changed when she went from W2 to owner draws in Q2, and the safe harbor calculation reset. Explain that to her. She runs a dog grooming business, she's smart, and she has no interest in tax mechanics. Three short paragraphs maximum. Don't use the phrase safe harbor. No cheerleading and no metaphors.

IT

Short version: your income did not change, but the way you get paid did, and that changed how the payments are calculated.

Until June you were on payroll, which meant taxes came out of every paycheck automatically. Since you switched to taking owner draws, nothing is being withheld. The money still has to get paid, so it moves from being taken out quietly to being paid by you directly four times a year. Same total, different route.

On top of that, last year's payment amount was set using a shortcut based on your prior year return. That shortcut expired when your setup changed, so this year's number is being calculated on what you are actually earning rather than on last year's number. It looks like an increase. It is really just an accurate number replacing an estimate.

That's something you can send. And notice what it didn't do. It didn't dumb the content down or make it vague. Every fact in there is a fact you gave it. It changed the route, not the destination.

The instruction that did the work was "she runs a dog grooming business, she's smart, and she has no interest in tax mechanics." That sentence tells it three separate things: her context, her capability, and her appetite. Without it you get either a technical answer or a condescending one, and the first attempt managed both.

Get specific about who's on the other end. "Explain this simply" produces mush. "Explain this to a sixty year old contractor who left school at seventeen, runs an eight million dollar business, and will be annoyed if you talk down to him" produces something you can send.

Example two: run it backwards

This is the move almost nobody thinks of and it's the best thing in this chapter.

Instead of asking it to write the explanation, write the explanation yourself, then hand it over and ask what will go wrong.

This one is a general contractor sending a note about a change order, because the failure is easier to see in someone else's trade than in your own.

YOU

Here's a paragraph I'm about to send to a homeowner. Don't rewrite it. Tell me what she's likely to misunderstand, what question she'll ask after reading it, and whether there's anything in here she could reasonably read as bad news when it isn't.

"Per the revised scope, the framing package will reflect the engineered beam substitution we discussed. There may be a variance in how this carries through the remaining draw schedule, but the contract sum is unchanged. Let me know if you have questions."

IT

What she will misunderstand. "Engineered beam substitution" and "draw schedule" are both terms she will read as vaguely alarming without knowing why. "Variance" is the third, and it is the worst of them, because in normal English a variance is a problem. Three unfamiliar words in two sentences is enough to make a reader stop processing meaning and start scanning for threat.

The question she will ask. Some version of "is this going to cost me more?" You never answer that, and it is the only thing she cares about.

What reads as bad news. "There may be a variance" is the line. To you that is a neutral note about timing. To her, "may be" plus a word she does not understand equals uncertainty about money, on a project where she is already braced for it. She will read that sentence three times.

Also, "the contract sum is unchanged" is doing the reassurance work in your paragraph, but it is buried in the second half of a sentence that starts with the scary part, so she will not get there.

The missing sentence. Whatever the answer is to "does this change my price," say it first and in dollars.

That's better feedback than most people get from a colleague, and it took eight seconds.

Use this on anything that matters. The fee letter from Chapter 5. The engagement letter. The treatment plan. The email you're slightly nervous about. It's a second pair of eyes that has read a hundred thousand examples of client communication going wrong.

Notice that nothing in that exchange required it to know anything about framing or engineered lumber. It knew what an unfamiliar word does to a reader. That transfers to every trade there is. Here's a pro tip, if you have access to more than one AI engine, send it to the second engine and ask it to critique the results from the first.

Example three: build it once

Some explanations you give constantly to different people, at different levels.

Build the whole set once.

YOU

I explain the difference between a bookkeeper, an accountant, and a fractional finance lead about twice a month, because prospects don't know what they're actually shopping for. Write me three versions of this explanation. One for a two person startup that has never had any of the three. One for a fifteen million dollar company with a bookkeeper who is over their head and doesn't know it. One I can put on my website that doesn't read as a sales pitch. Same facts, three audiences.

IT

For the two person startup

Right now you need one thing: someone to keep the record straight so that later on, anyone looking at your numbers can trust them. That is bookkeeping. It is not glamorous and it is not expensive, and skipping it is the single most common thing that costs founders money two years later when they are trying to raise or sell.

You do not need an accountant yet beyond your annual return. You definitely do not need a finance lead. Get the records clean and come back to us in eighteen months.

For the fifteen million dollar company

[it continues, framed around the specific failure mode of outgrowing a bookkeeper without noticing, careful not to insult the incumbent]

For the website

[a neutral third person version, no first person, no call to action]

That's one request. You now have a piece of collateral you were never going to sit down and write.

Then save it. Same principle as Chapter 5. The explanations worth having are worth keeping, and in Chapter 11 we'll cover turning your best ones into something the tool reaches for automatically.

WHAT TO WATCH FOR

You supply the facts. Every time.

This is the sharpest edge in the book and it's worth being blunt about. Notice that in example one, every fact came from the request. The safe harbor, the withholding change, the timing. It didn't know any of that. It translated what you told it.

The moment you invert that, you're in the danger zone from Chapter 4. "Explain to my client how the new depreciation rules work" is a request for it to supply the substance, and it'll supply something confident, well written, and possibly wrong. Your name goes on it either way.

Give it the facts, take back the words. That's the trade, and if you keep to it, this chapter is close to risk free.

Simple isn't the same as vague. Sometimes the plain version comes back having quietly dropped the qualification that mattered. "Your position is unchanged" is clean and might be true only under conditions you didn't mention. Read the simplified version specifically checking whether anything true got lost in the smoothing.

Don't over-explain to smart people. It has a mild tendency to pad, adding a friendly framing sentence and a reassuring closer. For a client who's sharper than you're giving them credit for, that reads as being handled. Say "no throat clearing, no reassurance at the end" when you want it flat.

DO THIS NOW

Take the last real explanation you sent a client. Pull it out of your sent folder.

Don't ask for a rewrite. Paste it in and ask example two's question: what will they misunderstand, what will they ask next, and what could read as bad news when it isn't.

Whatever comes back, that's the thing your clients have been quietly not understanding for years.

CHAPTER 8

Working With Numbers and Lists

“

Numbers tell you what happened.
Clarity tells you what to do next.

AI helps you turn messy data into insights
you can understand and act on.

CHAPTER 8

Working With Numbers and Lists

It's nine at night on a Tuesday and you have two lists open.

One is what your system says you invoiced last quarter. The other is what the client's accounts payable department says they received. They disagree by $4,180. You have been at this for an hour, you have checked the same six rows four times, and you have reached the stage where you are no longer reading the numbers so much as looking at them.

You already know how this ends. You'll find it eventually, or you'll write off the difference and feel bad about it.

That hour is the subject of this chapter, along with the formula you can never remember and the client list four different people have been wrecking since 2019.

I've put this in the middle of Part Two rather than at the front, because it needs Chapter 4. Numbers are the one area where this tool has a specific, well documented weakness, and using it on numbers without understanding that weakness is how careful people get burned. So we start with the rule that makes everything else here safe.

The rule

From Chapter 4: it doesn't calculate. It guesses what a calculated answer looks like.

For a column of forty figures with cents, it produces a number of roughly the right size that's wrong in a way you won't notice. That's the worst kind of wrong.

The fix takes six words.

Use code to calculate this.

Say that, and instead of guessing at the arithmetic, it writes and runs a small program. Same interface, same box, no programming knowledge required on your part. You'll usually see a note that code ran, which makes the calculation visible and reproducible.

Code fixes arithmetic, not a misunderstood instruction or messy input. Before you use the result, ask it to restate the calculation, confirm the row count and columns it used, show the formula or logic, and reconcile one spot-check or independent total. The code makes the work auditable. Your review makes it trustworthy.

Some versions now invoke code on their own for numeric work. Don't rely on that. Say the words and check what ran.

Everything in this chapter assumes you said the words. Write them on the sticky note next to "would I know if this were wrong."

Getting the data in and out

One practical thing first, because it's the wall people hit in the first four minutes and nobody mentions it.

You have a spreadsheet. It's on your machine. How does it get into a box on a web page?

Three ways, easiest first.

Drag the file in. Take the .xlsx straight from your folder and drop it into the chat window. All of them accept this now. This is the one to use, and it handles multiple tabs.

Copy and paste the cells. Select the range in Excel, copy, click in the box, paste. The columns arrive intact. Good for a few hundred rows, awkward past that.

Save as a CSV file and drag that in. Only worth doing if a file is misbehaving. It strips formatting and formulas, which is sometimes exactly what you want.

Coming back the other way is the part people don't expect. Ask for it as a table and you can select the result and paste it straight into a sheet, and the columns land in columns. Or ask it plainly: "give me that as a file I can open in Excel." It'll produce one you can download.

None of this requires anything to be connected to anything. You are moving a copy of your data into a chat window and moving a result back out, by hand, both directions. Which is worth remembering when we get to the part about what shouldn't go in.

Example one: the formula

The clearest, fastest win available. You know what you want the spreadsheet to do. You can't remember the syntax, and the last time you looked it up you lost eleven minutes to a forum post from 2014.

YOU

I have a sheet. Column A is client name, column B is invoice date, column C is amount, column D is date paid, blank if unpaid. I want a column that tells me how many days each invoice took to get paid, blank if it's still open, and I want a cell somewhere that gives me the average days to pay for the last twelve months only. Give me the formulas and tell me where to put them.

IT

Days to pay, put this in E2 and fill down:

```
=IF(D2="","",D2-B2)
```

Format the column as a number, not a date. Excel will try to make it a date and show you something like 01/12/1900. That is the most common thing that goes wrong here.

Average for the last twelve months, put this anywhere:

```
=AVERAGEIFS(E:E,B:B,">="&EDATE(TODAY(),-12),E:E,"<>")
```

That averages column E, counting only rows where the invoice date is within the last twelve months and where E is not blank.

One thing to check. This uses invoice date to decide what counts as the last twelve months. If you would rather go by payment date, swap B:B for D:D in the middle condition. Those give different answers and which one you want depends on the question you are asking.

Two minutes, including the formatting gotcha that would have cost you five minutes on its own.

The inverse is just as useful. You inherit a workbook. There's a formula in it that nobody understands and the person who built it left in 2022.

YOU

Explain what this does in plain English and tell me what breaks it.

=IFERROR(INDEX($H$2:$H$400,MATCH(1,($B$2:$B$400=A2)*($C$2:$C$400<=D2),0)),"CHECK")

IT

It is a two condition lookup. Reading it from the inside out: it walks down rows 2 through 400 looking for the first row where column B matches the value in A2 and column C is less than or equal to D2. When it finds that row, it returns the matching value from column H. If it finds nothing, it prints CHECK instead of an error.

In business terms it is probably matching a record to the most recent entry on or before a given date. A rate table lookup, or a price effective as of a date.

What breaks it:

- It only looks at rows 2 through 400. Add row 401 and it silently ignores it. This is the failure you should expect, and it will not throw an error, it will just print CHECK or return a stale value.
- It takes the first match, not the closest one. If your source data is not sorted the way the original author assumed, it returns the wrong row while looking perfectly fine.
- On older Excel versions this needs Ctrl+Shift+Enter to work. If it is returning odd results in one place and not another, check that.

If you want, tell me what the columns actually contain and I will tell you whether it is doing what you think it is doing.

That's a colleague who reads formulas fluently, available at ten at night.

Example two: the messy list

Every business has one. The client list that three people have added to over six years, with no rules.

YOU

Here's a client list that's been maintained by four different people. Clean it up. Standardize the name formatting, make the phone numbers consistent, flag anything that looks like a duplicate, and flag anything that looks wrong. Don't delete anything. Show me what you changed so I can check it. Use code so you don't miss rows.

[drops in the file, 340 rows]

IT

Processed 340 rows. Output below, changes marked.

Name formatting. 61 rows changed. Standardized to Last, First. The main issue was inconsistent handling of business names versus individuals. I left business names alone and only reformatted where the entry was clearly a person.

Phone numbers. 118 rows changed to (555) 555-5555 format. Six numbers had fewer than ten digits and I flagged rather than fixed them. Rows 44, 89, 156, 201, 288, 331.

Likely duplicates, 9 pairs. I did not merge these, only flagged them:

- Rows 12 and 207: "Ramirez Construction" and "Ramirez Construction LLC", same phone
- Rows 55 and 298: "Bob Kellner" and "Robert Kellner", same address, different phone
- Rows 91 and 92: identical except one has a middle initial - [six more]

Things that look wrong, 7 rows.

- Row 73: email is "same as above". Needs a human.
- Row 118: state is "FL" with a trailing space, which will break any filter you run
- Row 145: zip code is 4 digits
- Row 230: this looks like a note someone typed into the wrong field. It says "call before 10, hates voicemail" - [three more]

What I did not touch. 14 rows have blank email. That may be intentional so I left them.

Row 230 is the one I want you to notice. Somebody's useful institutional knowledge, typed into the wrong cell in 2019, invisible to everyone since. Every messy list has three or four of those.

The instruction that matters is "don't delete anything, show me what you changed." Never let it clean data silently. You want the change log, because you're going to spot check twenty rows before you trust the other three hundred and twenty.

Example three: the reconciliation

Back to Tuesday night and the $4,180.

I'm going to show you this one twice, because the first version is the mistake I still catch myself making and it's the whole reason this chapter opens with six words.

YOU

Two lists. The first is what our system says we invoiced in Q3. The second is what the client's accounts payable says they received. They disagree by $4,180 and I've been staring at this for an hour. Find the difference.

IT

I found the discrepancy. Here is the breakdown.

In your list, not theirs. 4 items, $6,240 total. Invoices 3318 ($1,200), 3341 ($2,750), 3390 ($1,890), and 3391 ($500).

In their list, not yours. 1 item, $2,100. Reference INV-3299, dated June 29.

Amount mismatch. 1 item. Invoice 3355 shows $4,400 on your side and $4,340 on theirs, a $60 difference.

Net difference: $6,240 minus $2,100 plus $60 equals $4,200. That is within $20 of your stated gap of $4,180, so this accounts for the discrepancy. The small remainder is likely a rounding difference.

Look at that. It found the items, it produced a clean total, and it landed within twenty dollars of the number you already had. You'd close the laptop.

Add up those four invoices yourself. $1,200 plus $2,750 plus $1,890 plus $500 is $6,340, not $6,240.

It was off by a hundred dollars, and because it was off by a hundred dollars, its final number came out closer to what you expected. The wrong arithmetic made the answer look more confirmed than the right arithmetic would have. That's not a freak occurrence. That's the failure mode doing exactly what Chapter 4 said it does, and the reason it's dangerous is sitting right there in your reaction to it.

Now with the six words.

YOU

Do that again and use code to calculate it. Show me every item that's in one list and not the other, and every item in both where the amount differs. Give me the totals from the code, not from your head.

IT

Reconciled 84 items against 81. Here is the entire discrepancy.

In your list, not theirs. 4 items, $6,340 total.

Invoice	**Date**	**Amount**
3318	Jul 14	$1,200
3341	Aug 2	$2,750
3390	Sep 28	$1,890
3391	Sep 30	$500

In their list, not yours. 1 item, $2,100.

Reference	**Date**	**Amount**
INV-3299	Jun 29	$2,100

In both, amounts differ. 1 item.

Invoice	**Yours**	**Theirs**	**Difference**
3355	$4,400	$4,340	$60

Net: $6,340 minus $2,100 plus $60 equals $4,300. Your stated gap is $4,180, a $120 difference, so one of us has a rounding or transcription issue somewhere. Worth resolving before you send this.

Two patterns worth noting. Invoices 3390 and 3391 are both from the last three days of the quarter, which points at a cutoff timing difference rather than a real dispute. And INV-3299 is dated June 29, which is Q2, so it may be correctly excluded from your list and incorrectly included in theirs.

Under a minute for the hour. And notice the difference in what you walk away with.

The first version told you the mystery was solved. The second one told you there's still $120 unaccounted for, which means there's a real error somewhere in one of the two systems and you'd have shipped it. The honest answer is less satisfying and worth considerably more.

The last paragraph is the part a spreadsheet can't give you, because it isn't comparison, it's a read on what the pattern means.

WHAT TO WATCH FOR

Test it on something you already know. Before you trust it on live work, run it against a reconciliation you already completed by hand. Give it the two lists, let it work, compare it to your answer. Ten minutes, once. That single test is worth more than any assurance I can give you in a book.

Real client data doesn't go in. This is where the rules in Chapter 12 bite hardest, because this chapter is the most tempting place to break them. A client list with names, addresses, and tax numbers is exactly the thing you shouldn't paste into a free consumer account.

Two ways through it. Pay for the business version, which is rule two in Chapter 12 and largely why that rule exists. Or strip the identifying columns before you paste, since it doesn't need real names to find your duplicates. Client 001 through Client 340 works just as well.

Watch for the confident total. You just saw it. If you forget the six words and it does arithmetic in its head, the answer arrives with exactly the same confidence as a calculated one. There's no visual difference between a real total and a guessed one. The only defense is the habit.

It can't see your actual file. Everything here works on data you pasted in or a file you dropped in. It isn't connected to your accounting system and it isn't watching your workbook. Some tools offer that kind of connection, and they are worth looking at eventually. That is a conversation for The AI Owner's Manual.

DO THIS NOW

Open the spreadsheet you use most.

Find the thing in it you always do by hand. The manual sort, the copy paste between tabs, the formula you gave up on and now work around.

Describe it in plain English, exactly as you would to a person sitting next to you, and end with "use code to calculate this."

If you only ever use this tool for one thing, this is a strong candidate for the one thing.

CHAPTER 9

Using It to Think Out Loud

The best ideas rarely appear fully formed.
They emerge through conversation—first with yourself.

AI gives you a sounding board that challenges assumptions, opens new angles, and helps you find the ideas you might not reach on your own.

CHAPTER 9

Using It to Think Out Loud

You have to let someone go on Thursday.

You've been running the conversation in your head since Sunday. In the shower, on the drive, at two in the morning. Every version goes differently and none of them go well. You can't practice it on your spouse because they know the person. You can't practice it on your management team because one of them will let something slip. You can't practice it on your peer group because the next meeting is in three weeks and Thursday is Thursday.

So you'll walk in cold, having rehearsed it forty times alone and never once out loud.

This chapter is about that gap. It's the least obvious use in this book and the one that has surprised the most owners I've handed it to, because it isn't about output at all. Nothing here produces a document. What it produces is a better version of your own thinking, arrived at faster.

Example one: the rehearsal

YOU

I have to let someone go Thursday and I want to practice. Here's the situation. Eight years with us, well liked, and his work has been slipping for about eighteen months. We've had three documented conversations. He has a kid starting college. I'm not looking for reassurance that I'm doing the right thing, I've made the decision. I want to practice saying it.

Play him. Respond the way a person actually responds, not the way a training video does. Push back on me. I'll start.

"Dave, thanks for coming in. I need to talk to you about something difficult, and I want to be direct with you rather than dance around it."

IT

"Okay." [he sits down, does not take off his jacket] "This is about the Henderson thing, isn't it. Look, I know that got away from me, but I told Marie I was going to have it cleaned up by Friday and I meant it."

YOU

"It's not about Henderson specifically. Dave, we're ending your employment here. Today is your last day."

IT

[long pause] "You're firing me."

[another pause] "Eight years. Eight years, and you're doing this in April. You know Katie starts in the fall. You know that."

"Was this Marie? Because if this is about Marie I want to say something, and I should have said it six months ago."

That's the moment you haven't rehearsed. You planned the opening. You didn't plan for him to pivot to blaming a colleague, and you didn't plan for him to say the word "Katie" out loud.

Keep going. Say the wrong thing on purpose and see what it costs. Then back up and try it a different way. Run the whole thing three times. It takes about ten minutes and you'll walk in Thursday having already lived through the version that goes badly.

This works for anything you're dreading. The partner conversation you've been avoiding for two years. Telling a client you're resigning the engagement. Telling a patient the crown they've had for six years failed because of something you missed. Standing in a driveway telling a homeowner the job needs another eleven thousand dollars of work nobody found until the deck came off. The negotiation where you have to say a number out loud that feels too high.

Tell it who to play, tell it to be realistic rather than cooperative, and go.

Example two: the decision you keep circling

Some decisions aren't hard because they're complicated. They're hard because you've been thinking about them alone.

YOU

I'm going back and forth on hiring a second senior person. Don't give me a framework and don't give me a list of pros and cons. I want you to interview me. Ask me one question at a time, wait for my answer, and go where my answers take you. Dig into anything that sounds like I'm avoiding it.

IT

What happens on the day you do not hire anyone and everything continues exactly as it is now for another two years?

YOU

Honestly, it works. It's tight, but it works. I'd be doing more client work than I want to.

IT

You said "more client work than I want to" rather than "more than I should." Which is it? Those point at different decisions.

YOU

...both, probably. I'm the bottleneck on about a third of the accounts and I don't enjoy that part of it anymore.

IT

So there are two problems here and you have been treating them as one. One is capacity, which a hire solves. The other is that you have stopped enjoying a specific kind of work, which a hire only solves if you hire someone who takes that work specifically.

When you have imagined this hire, which of those two problems were you imagining them solving?

That's a real question. It's the question a good advisor asks, and it took four exchanges instead of a scheduled meeting.

The instruction that makes this work is "ask me one question at a time." Left alone it'll produce a thorough, balanced, entirely useless analysis of hiring decisions in general. Told to interview you, it works on your actual situation, and the value comes from your own answers rather than from anything it knows.

Example three: make it argue

Here's the honest warning this chapter exists to deliver, and I want to show it to you rather than describe it.

Same plan, asked the normal way.

YOU

I'm thinking about buying the building we currently lease. Asking is $1.4 million, we pay $94,000 a year in rent, I've been here eleven years and expect to be here another fifteen. Financing at current rates works out roughly even against rent in year one and better every year after. Is my reasoning sound?

IT

Your reasoning is sound, and the fundamentals here are solid. A few thoughts:

What is working in your favor. An eleven year tenancy tells you this location works for your business, which removes most of the uncertainty that makes commercial purchases risky. Converting rent into equity is a well established way for an owner operated business to build balance sheet value, and if the year one comparison is already roughly even, the arithmetic improves every year as rent would have escalated and your payment does not.

A few considerations. You will want to budget for maintenance and capital items that your landlord currently handles. It is also worth confirming the property is priced in line with comparable buildings in the area, and having a conversation with your lender about rate structure.

Overall. Given your time horizon and your history in the space, this appears to be a reasonable move. The main question is whether the capital outlay is a comfortable fit alongside your other plans for the business.

Notice what happened. It agreed with you, in an organized and intelligent way, and it produced the feeling of having your thinking checked without checking anything.

The considerations paragraph is the tell. Every item in it is a thing you would obviously do anyway. Budget for maintenance. Check comps. Talk to the lender. Nothing in there could stop you, and nothing in there names a risk you hadn't already thought of.

It's agreeable by default. Present it with your plan and it'll find the merits. Ask if your reasoning is sound and it'll usually say yes, with a couple of gentle considerations at the end. It's built to be helpful, and in most contexts helpful reads as supportive.

That's fine for drafting an email. It's dangerous when you're making a decision, because agreeable feedback on a bad plan feels exactly like validation.

You have to explicitly break it.

YOU

Start over and argue against it as hard as you can, the way a smart competitor or a skeptical board member would. Don't tell me what's good about it. Find the assumption I haven't examined. If you think the plan is fine, say so, but don't soften anything to be nice.

IT

The strongest argument against is not financial, so let me deal with the financial one first and then get to the real objection.

Financially, "roughly even in year one" is doing a lot of work. That comparison almost certainly excludes the things a landlord currently absorbs. Roof, air conditioning replacement, structural, property tax reassessment on sale, insurance, and the maintenance you do not currently think about because you call someone. On a building at that price, budget one to two percent of value annually for those. That is $14,000 to $28,000 a year that is not in your comparison, and it is lumpy, arriving as a $40,000 roof in a year you did not plan for one.

Now the real objection.

You said you expect to be here fifteen more years. What you have not said is what happens to this business when you stop. If the plan is to sell, you are about to make your business harder to sell by tying it to a specific building, and you are converting liquid capacity into an illiquid asset in the decade before you need flexibility most.

If the plan is to hand it to someone internally, you have created a second transaction they have to finance on top of the first.

The unexamined assumption is not about interest rates. It is that the next fifteen years look like the last eleven. You have eleven years of evidence that you like this building. You have zero evidence about whether your firm needs a building in 2035.

Same plan. Same tool. Same conversation, two messages apart.

The first response mentioned maintenance as a thing to budget for. The second one put a number on it and pointed out that the number is missing from your comparison. And the first response never got anywhere near your succession plan, which is the actual issue.

Whether or not it's right is beside the point. It found the thing you weren't looking at, which is the entire job. Getting there required one sentence of instruction, and without that sentence you'd have walked away feeling checked.

WHAT TO WATCH FOR

It isn't a substitute for the room.

I want to be direct about this because it's the failure mode I'd most regret contributing to. It's available at eleven at night, it never gets tired of the topic, and it never judges you. For an owner, who is often short of people to think out loud with, that combination is seductive.

It's a rehearsal space. It isn't your peer group, your board, your attorney, or your spouse. It has no stake in the outcome, no memory of your last three decisions, and no ability to tell you that you've said this exact thing every year since 2021. The people in your life who can do that are doing something categorically different, and this makes that more valuable rather than less, because you walk into those conversations having already done the first pass.

Use it to prepare for the room. Don't use it instead of the room.

Watch the agreement. If you notice you feel good after every session, something is wrong. Real thinking partners make you uncomfortable sometimes. Build the habit of asking it to argue the other side, every time, on anything that matters.

It doesn't know you. In example two it asked a good question, but it asked it without knowing you tried this hire in 2019 and it went badly. It can't factor in what you don't tell it. The quality of what comes back is capped by how honestly you describe your own situation, which is a harder discipline than it sounds.

DO THIS NOW

Think of the conversation you're currently dreading. There is one.

Tell it the situation in five sentences, tell it who to play, tell it to be realistic rather than cooperative, and say your opening line.

Then let it be difficult. The whole value is in the part that doesn't go how you planned.

CHAPTER 10

Making Small Things That Save You Time

You don't need to automate everything.
Just the things you do over and over.

AI helps you build simple templates and automations that eliminate busywork so you can focus on what actually moves your business forward.

CHAPTER 10

Making Small Things That Save You Time

Everything so far has been disposable.

The fee letter got sent. The lease got read. The reconciliation got done. All of it was useful and none of it exists anymore. Tomorrow there's a different letter and a different lease.

This chapter is different. Everything in it produces something that keeps working after you close the tab.

Small things. A checklist. A form. A one page diagram. Nobody writes a book chapter about checklists, which is exactly why every business is full of processes that live in one person's head and get done slightly differently every time. Not because anyone decided that was fine. Because writing it down was a two hour job that never got to the top of the list.

It's now a nine minute job. That changes what's worth documenting.

Example one: get it out of your head

The thing you know how to do and have never written down.

The trick isn't to try to write it. You'll do a bad job, because you've done it four hundred times and the parts you'd forget to mention are exactly the parts a new person needs. Instead, let it interview you.

YOU

I need to document our new client onboarding process. It exists entirely in my head and my office manager's head, and she's retiring in November. Don't write the document yet. Interview me first. Ask one question at a time, and when I skip a step because it's obvious to me, catch it.

IT

Start at the very beginning. A new client says yes. What is the first thing that physically happens, and who does it?

YOU

Marie sets up the file and sends the engagement letter.

IT

Sets up the file where, and does she need anything from you before she can? You said "sets up the file" as though it is one action, and it usually is not.

YOU

In the practice management system. She needs the engagement type and the fee, which I usually just tell her verbally.

IT

So there is an undocumented handoff there that only works because you and Marie are in the same office and you tell her out loud. That is one of the things that will break in November. Noted, we will come back to it.

Next: the engagement letter. Is it a template she fills in, or does it get customized, and who signs off before it goes out?

Fifteen minutes of that and it has more of the process than you could have written in two hours, including the four handoffs that only work because two specific people sit near each other.

Then:

YOU

Okay, that's everything. Now write it up. Two versions. One is a checklist Marie's replacement can follow literally, step by step, with nothing assumed. The other is a one page overview for me, so I can see where the process actually breaks.

The second document is the one you didn't know you needed. It comes back with the verbal handoff, the unnamed approval step, and the point where three different people all think someone else is checking something.

This works on anything undocumented. Month end close. Quoting a job. How a work order gets from the phone to the shop floor. What happens when a machine goes down at four in the afternoon. How a new patient goes from phone call to seated in a chair with a completed history. The interview is the whole technique, and it works because it's genuinely hard to describe your own expertise from a blank page and easy to answer a question.

Example two: the form you never made

Every business has an intake conversation it improvises, and every business has the story of the job that went sideways because nobody asked the one question.

YOU

Build me an intake form for prospective clients. Context: we're an eleven person accounting firm, we take on small businesses between about two and thirty million in revenue. The three things that have burned us historically are clients who are behind on filings and don't mention it, clients whose books are in much worse shape than they describe, and clients who are shopping purely on price and will leave in a year.

Design the questions so those three things surface without me having to ask about them directly. People won't answer "are your books a mess" honestly. Keep it under fifteen questions.

IT

New Client Intake

Basics

- Business name, entity type, state of formation, and year founded
- Approximate annual revenue
- Number of employees

Current state, phrased to surface reality 4. Who currently handles your bookkeeping, and how long have they been doing it? 5. When was your last completed month end close? (Month and year) 6. What is the date of the most recent tax return you have filed? 7. If we asked for a profit and loss statement for last month today, how long would it take you to get it to us?

Fit and expectations 8. What prompted you to look for a new accountant right now? 9. Who else are you talking to? 10. What did not work about your last arrangement? 11. What would need to be true a year from now for you to say this was worth it?

[four more]

Why questions 5, 6, and 7 are phrased that way. Nobody says their books are a mess. Everybody can answer a date question, and a date question is not an accusation. If question 5 comes back "uh, sometime last spring" you have your answer without anyone having to admit anything.

Question 7 is the strongest single question on this form. The answer is almost always honest, because the person is imagining actually doing it.

Question 8 is your price shopper detector. "Our guy retired" is a different client from "we thought we were paying too much." Both are fine. They are not the same sale.

That form now runs your intake for the next five years and it cost you four minutes.

The same request works for a contractor's site visit checklist, a shop's work order form, or the questions a service manager should be asking before quoting. Name the three ways jobs have gone wrong on you and let it design backwards from those.

Example three: draw the thing

Some explanations only work as a picture, and most owners have quietly accepted they'll never have the picture, because making one means either learning software or paying someone.

You can just ask. But the first ask usually comes back wrong in a specific way, and it's worth seeing why.

YOU

Make me a diagram showing how a document moves through our office, from client upload to filed return. The steps are: client uploads to portal, Marie checks it is complete, it goes to a preparer, then to me for review, then back to the client for signature, then filed. Show the two loops where things bounce back, which are Marie sending it back to the client for missing documents, and me sending it back to the preparer for corrections.

IT

[produces a diagram: eleven boxes of equal size, each holding a full sentence of text, arranged in a grid. The two return loops are drawn as long lines that cross the main flow twice. A legend at the bottom explains three arrow styles.]

Everything you asked for is in there. It's still no good.

The boxes are all the same size, so nothing looks more important than anything else. The text inside them is too long to read at a glance, which defeats the point of a diagram. And the return loops cross the main flow, which is the visual equivalent of a sentence you have to read twice.

None of that is a failure to follow instructions. You told it what to include. You never told it what the thing is for.

YOU

Too busy. This is going to be printed on one page and pinned to the wall next to Marie's desk, and people will glance at it for two seconds while walking past. Redo it. Three or four words per box maximum, no legend, no crossing lines. Make the main flow a single straight line left to right so it reads like a sentence, and hang the two bounce-back loops underneath it so they're clearly the exception rather than part of the path.

IT

produces a second diagram: six short boxes in a straight horizontal line, three words each. Two curved arrows loop back underneath, each labeled with two words. Nothing crosses. Maybe it looks like ...

That one you can print.

The instruction that fixed it wasn't about content. It was "printed on one page, pinned to a wall, glanced at for two seconds." Tell it where the thing is going to live and who's looking at it, and the format decisions make themselves. That's the same move as Chapter 7's "she runs a dog grooming business and has no interest in tax mechanics," pointed at a picture instead of a paragraph.

Is it as good as a designer's? No. Is it better than the nothing you've had for eleven years? By a distance.

The same applies to a simple org chart, a one page process map, a rough floor plan for the office move, or a chart that makes a number land in a partner meeting. These are all places where the gap between nothing and something rough is enormous, and the gap between something rough and something polished is small and mostly doesn't matter.

Where the picture earns its keep is Chapter 7 territory. Take the explanation you built for clients and ask for the one page visual version. Some clients will never read three paragraphs and will absorb the whole thing from a diagram in eight seconds.

WHAT TO WATCH FOR

Documenting a broken process gives you a documented broken process. The interview in example one will surface things that are wrong. When it says "there is an undocumented verbal handoff there," that isn't a formatting note. Fix the process, then document it. Otherwise you've just made the mess durable and given it authority.

Nobody uses a checklist that's too long. It'll happily produce forty steps because you asked for thorough. A forty step checklist gets read once and abandoned. Ask for the version that fits on one page and put the detail in a separate reference document that nobody reads and everybody is glad exists.

These need owners and dates. A document nobody owns is stale within a year and actively misleading within two, and a stale checklist is worse than none because people follow it. Put a name and a review date at the bottom of every single thing you make in this chapter. That one line is the difference between an asset and future confusion.

Keep them somewhere real. Not in the chat history. Not in your downloads folder. Wherever your business actually keeps documents, on the day you make them. Everything in this chapter is worthless if you can't find it in March.

DO THIS NOW

Name the process that lives entirely in one person's head. Every business has at least one and you thought of it before you finished this sentence.

Start the interview. Don't write anything yourself. Just answer questions for fifteen minutes and then ask for the two documents.

If that person is retiring, quitting, or has been talking about slowing down, do it this week rather than this month.

CHAPTER 11

Teaching It How You Work

The more you teach it about you, the more valuable it becomes.

AI adapts to your preferences, your tone, and your priorities—so every interaction starts closer to what you need.

CHAPTER 11

Teaching It How You Work

By now something small has probably started to annoy you.

Every chapter in this part has told you to give it context. Who the client is, how you write, what your firm does, what you're trying to accomplish. That advice is correct and it's the difference between useless output and useful output.

It's also four sentences you've now typed roughly two hundred times.

That friction isn't a minor irritation. It's the thing that decides whether you're still using this in six months. People don't quit because it stopped working. They quit because every single task started from zero, and starting from zero forty times a week is exhausting in a way that eventually loses to just doing it yourself.

This chapter fixes that. It's the last chapter of Part Two and it's the one that converts a tool you use into a tool that works the way your firm works.

Remember the new hire from Chapter 1. Everything you've done so far has been re-explaining your business to them every single morning, because they arrive with no memory of yesterday. This chapter is the part where you finally write it down and hand it to them.

Three layers. Do them in order, and the whole thing takes under an hour.

Layer one: tell it who you are, once

Every one of these tools has a place to put standing instructions. It lives in the settings and it's called something like custom instructions, preferences, or personalization. Find it. It's the single most underused feature in any of them.

Whatever you put there gets applied to every conversation, forever, without you typing it again.

Most people either never find it or write something like this.

Standing instructions: Be professional and concise. Write in a business appropriate tone. Be helpful and accurate.

Then they go back to work and nothing changes, and they conclude the feature doesn't do much.

Of course nothing changed. Every one of those words describes what it was already trying to do. "Be professional" is not an instruction, it's a compliment. "Concise" without a length is a preference it will quietly average away. And "accurate" is a wish.

Standing instructions only bite when they're specific enough that you could tell whether they were followed. Here's the way to get there without writing them yourself.

YOU

I want to write standing instructions so I stop repeating myself. Interview me. Ask about how I write, what I hate, what my business is, and anything else that would change your output. Then draft the instructions.

Fifteen questions later you get something like this:

IT

About me and my business I am a partner at an eleven person accounting firm in South Florida. Our clients are small businesses, roughly two to thirty million in revenue, mostly construction, trades, and professional services. I have been doing this for twenty two years.

How I write Short. I get to the point in the first sentence. I do not use greetings like "I hope this finds you well" and I do not use closing pleasantries. I sign off with my first name only. I would rather sound blunt than sound corporate.

What to never do

- Do not open with a restatement of my question
- Do not use the words delve, leverage, robust, or streamline
- Do not end with an offer to help further unless I asked for one
- Do not use bullet points unless the content is genuinely a list
- Do not soften bad news into vagueness

Default behavior

- When I ask for something written, give me one version, not three, unless I ask
- When numbers are involved, use code to calculate rather than working it out in your head
- If my request is missing something you need, ask me rather than guessing
- If you think I am wrong, say so directly

Read the two side by side. The first one is four adjectives. The second one contains a business, a signature convention, four banned words, and a standing order about arithmetic. Every line in it could be checked.

Paste that into the settings. Every conversation from now on starts with it already known.

The difference is immediate and slightly startling. The first draft is suddenly 80 percent right instead of 50 percent right, because it's no longer guessing at things you never told it.

Notice that the "never do" list is the most valuable section. It's easier to describe what irritates you than what you want, and irritation is a reliable signal. Add to that list every time something comes back wrong in the same way twice.

Layer two: give it the facts it cannot know

Standing instructions cover how you communicate. Layer two covers what your business actually is.

Make one document. Call it whatever you want. Put in it the things you find yourself explaining over and over:

- What you do and what you deliberately don't do
- Your service tiers and roughly what they cost
- Your clients, described as types rather than names
- Your policies. Payment terms, turnaround times, what you won't do
- The recurring situations and how you handle each one
- Your team, roles, who handles what

- The things that make your firm different from the one down the road

Two pages is plenty. Then attach that document to any conversation where it matters, or better, put it into a saved space as described in layer three.

The change is that it stops giving you generic accounting firm answers and starts giving you answers about your firm.

YOU

[with the reference document attached] A prospect just asked if we do valuations for divorce proceedings. Draft my reply.

IT

We do not. That is one of the four things your document lists as deliberately out of scope, and the note says you refer those to Kessler.

Draft:

"We don't handle valuation work for litigation. It's a specialty and doing it occasionally is how people get themselves in trouble as expert witnesses.

Ken Kessler does this properly and I'd trust him with it. I'll make the introduction if you want.

Happy to help with anything on the accounting side either way.

Ray"

It caught the referral because you wrote it down once, three weeks ago.

Layer three: a room for the work you repeat

The third layer is for jobs that come around on a cycle.

Every one of these tools now has some version of a saved workspace. A project, a space, a folder. What matters isn't the name, it's that you can attach documents and instructions to it permanently and every conversation you start inside it already knows them.

Set one up for each thing you do repeatedly.

Client onboarding. Attach the intake form from Chapter 10, the engagement letter template, and the process checklist. Instructions: "When I paste in intake responses, flag anything concerning, draft the engagement letter, and tell me what to ask about on the follow up call."

Month end. Attach the close checklist and your reporting format. Instructions on what you want flagged and how you want the summary written.

Prospect responses. Attach the reference document and your three best explanations from Chapter 7.

Now the work starts at the third step instead of the first. You aren't describing the situation, you're handing over the input.

The compounding part

Here's what this looks like over a year, and it's why this chapter closes Part Two.

Month one you type everything from scratch. It's useful and it's effortful.

Month two you have standing instructions and the first drafts start landing close. Month four you have the reference document and it stops giving you answers that could apply to anyone. Month seven you have four saved spaces and the recurring work has stopped being work.

Month twelve, someone asks how you got so much out of this and you struggle to explain, because none of it was a big move. It was an hour spent on setup and then a habit of adding one line every time something came back wrong.

The people who get very little out of this tool and the people who get an enormous amount are, in my experience, using the identical software. The difference is entirely whether they spent that first hour.

WHAT TO WATCH FOR

No client information in standing instructions. Ever. Standing instructions apply to every conversation, which means anything you put there is in play permanently. Describe client types, never client names. The reference document is the same. This connects directly to Chapter 12, which is next, and it's one of the two places people get it wrong.

Instructions go stale and stale is worse than empty. Your prices change. Your policies change. Ken Kessler retires. Then it confidently tells a prospect to call a man who closed his practice in 2027. Put a calendar reminder for once a quarter, read your instructions and reference document, and update them. Ten minutes.

Don't over-instruct. There's a temptation, once this works, to keep adding rules until you have four pages of them. Past a point the instructions start fighting each other and the output gets stiff and strange. If you're past about a page, you've probably put task-specific things in a place meant for universal ones. Move those into the relevant saved space.

Universal means universal. Anything in your standing instructions applies when you're drafting a client letter and also when you're asking for a recipe on a Sunday. Keep them to things that are true regardless of what you're doing.

DO THIS NOW

Find the settings. Look for custom instructions, preferences, or personalization.

Then ask it to interview you and write the instructions for you. Don't try to write them yourself from a blank page, for exactly the reason Chapter 10 gave: describing your own habits cold is hard, and answering questions about them is easy.

Fifteen minutes. Then go back and redo the very first thing you tried in Chapter 3 and see how different it comes back.

That's the end of Part Two. You now know what this thing can do for your business. Part three is what it can do to your business if you're careless, and then Part Four is about making it stick.

PART THREE

The Four Rules

One chapter. Four rules. Eight minutes.

CHAPTER 12

Four Rules So You Don't Get Burned

"

Smart AI use isn't about going fast.
It's about staying safe as you go.

These four rules help you avoid common mistakes and build confidence—so AI becomes a strength for your business, not a risk.

CHAPTER 12

Four Rules So You Don't Get Burned

This is the shortest part of this book and it's one chapter long. That's deliberate.

Most books about AI for business open with risk. Policy, compliance, data governance, an acceptable use framework, a committee. I've read those books and I've watched what happens when an owner reads one. They come away convinced this is complicated and dangerous, they decide to sort out the governance first, and eighteen months later they have a policy document and nobody in the building has used the tool.

Meanwhile their staff have been using it on their phones the entire time.

So I put the risk chapter here, after eleven chapters of what it can do, because I wanted you to have your hands on it before anyone talked to you about rules. And I've kept it to four rules, because four is the number of things a person actually remembers.

Everything here fits on one page. The AI Owner's Manual has the full implementation treatment for anyone who needs it, and at the end of this chapter I'll tell you whether you're one of those people.

Start from the truth

Your people are already using it.

Not maybe. Almost certainly, and probably more of them than you'd guess. They're using it on their phones, with their personal email addresses, on the free tier, and they haven't told you because nobody asked and they weren't sure it was allowed.

This is worth sitting with for a second, because it inverts the usual framing. The question in front of you isn't whether to introduce AI into your business. It's already in your business. The question is whether it's going to happen on accounts you know about, on the paid tier, with four rules everyone has read, or on personal accounts you can't see.

That's the whole reason this chapter exists, and it's why rule four isn't optional.

Rule one

Assume anything you type could be read by someone else.

Not because it will be. Because that assumption produces exactly the right behavior with no further thinking required.

You don't need to understand data retention policies or model training to apply this. You already have this instinct. It's the same instinct that tells you what not to put in an email, and you've been applying it correctly for twenty years.

What stays out:

- Client tax numbers, account numbers, bank details
- Passwords or login credentials, ever, for any reason
- Anything covered by a confidentiality agreement you signed
- Employee medical or personal information
- Anything you wouldn't want read aloud in a deposition

What's fine, and this is most of your work:

- Your own drafts, letters, and documents
- Public information about anyone
- Client situations with the identifying details stripped out
- Your internal processes, checklists, and templates

And the practical workaround for much ordinary, nonregulated work: it often does not need real names. In Chapter 8 you cleaned a client list. That list works just as well with Client 001 through Client 340. Strip the identifying columns, do the work, and put the names back. This substantially reduces exposure, but it does not override a contract, privilege obligation, regulation, or a rule specific to your firm.

Rule two

Pay for the business version.

Use a company-managed business workspace when the information and team justify it. Pricing is usually per person, but minimum seats and required base subscriptions can make the true starting cost higher than the advertised seat price.

The reason is simple. Consumer services may use conversations to improve models depending on the provider and your settings. Business workspaces generally opt company data out by default and state that in writing. They also add administrative control. Those are real differences and among the highest-leverage choices in this chapter.

A business workspace also means the accounts belong to your company. You can see who has access and turn it off when someone leaves. A paid personal plan opened with a work email does not automatically provide that control.

I'm aware this is the one rule that costs money, and a rule that costs money always gets more scrutiny. Put it against the alternative: staff using personal accounts for company work, with no shared administration and data terms nobody reviewed. For a solo owner, a paid personal plan with the provider's training controls disabled may be a practical first step, but it is not a substitute for a managed workspace once a team or sensitive workflow is involved.

Also: read what you're agreeing to at signup. Start with whether your data may improve the model, how long it is retained, who administers the account, and what minimum commitment applies. The current plan comparison is at jesscoburn.com/resources/.

Rule three

Check anything that leaves your office with your name on it.

It drafts. You sign.

That's the entire rule and it isn't really an AI rule. Go back to the new hire from Chapter 1. Brilliant, fast, has read everything, has been at your firm for eleven minutes. You would not let their memo go to a client without reading it, and you wouldn't feel bad about that. Nothing changes here.

What changes is how easy it is to forget, because the output is polished. A junior person's rough draft announces that it needs review. A clean, well organized, confidently written document does not. Chapter 4 covered why that matters and gave you the two second test, which is the operational version of this rule.

Would I know if this were wrong?

Ask it before anything goes out the door. If the answer is no, you're verifying or you're not sending.

Nothing goes to a client, a regulator, or a court unread. Ever. If your work touches any of those three, that isn't a guideline.

Rule four

Tell your team what is okay, in one paragraph.

Not a policy. A paragraph. Here it is, and you should feel free to use it as written.

> We use AI tools here and you are encouraged to. Use the company account, not a personal one. Never put client identifying information into it, including names, account numbers, or anything from a signed confidentiality agreement. If you are unsure whether something counts, strip the names out or ask me. Everything it produces is a draft, so you are responsible for checking anything that goes out with our name on it. If it saves you time, tell me what you did so we can all use it.

Under a hundred words. Send it today.

Three things make it work.

It starts with permission. A paragraph that opens with a prohibition gets read as a ban regardless of what follows, and a ban drives usage back to personal phones where you can't see it.

It gives one clear line. No client identifying information. One rule to remember beats seven.

It ends with an invitation. The last sentence is the most valuable one in the paragraph. Someone in your business is about to find something useful, and whether they tell you is decided by whether you asked.

Whether you need more than this

Four rules cover the large majority of small businesses. Some of you need more, and I'd rather say so plainly than let you assume the paragraph is sufficient.

You need more than this chapter if:

- You're licensed by a body with its own technology or confidentiality requirements
- Your work carries a privilege obligation, meaning attorneys and some financial and medical practices
- You handle protected health information
- You have clients whose contracts specify how their data may be processed
- You're in a regulated industry with examination requirements

If any of those describe you, the four rules are still correct and still your starting point. They aren't the finish line. Talk to whoever handles your compliance. The AI Owner's Manual has the full treatment: data classification, vendor assessment, incident response, and an acceptable-use policy that is an actual policy rather than a paragraph.

Don't let that stop you starting. It means your version of rule four is longer, not that rules one through three change.

WHAT TO WATCH FOR

The paragraph isn't a filing exercise. Sending it once and never mentioning it again produces a paragraph nobody remembers. Bring it up when someone shows you something good. That's the moment it lands, because that's the moment people are paying attention.

Watch for the quiet drift. Month one everyone strips the names out. Month six someone is in a hurry. The drift is normal and the fix isn't enforcement, it's making the right way easier. If stripping names is painful for a common task, solve that, because a rule that makes work harder loses to the work every time.

Don't confuse this chapter with being finished. Four rules is the floor. It's a very good floor for a small business and it's dramatically better than the policy document nobody wrote. It's still a floor.

DO THIS NOW

Copy the paragraph. Change the parts that don't fit your business. Send it to your team today.

Then ask one question in your next staff meeting: who's already using this, and what for?

Ask it in a way that makes clear nobody's in trouble, because they aren't, and because the answers will tell you more about where the value is in your business than anything in the previous eleven chapters.

PART FOUR

Make It Stick

The part most people skip and shouldn't.

CHAPTER 13

Pick Your One Thing

Focus on one small win that makes a real difference.
Master it. Then build from there.

1. **LOOK AT YOUR LIST**

List the things that slow you down, frustrate you, or take too much time.

2. **CHOOSE YOUR ONE THING**

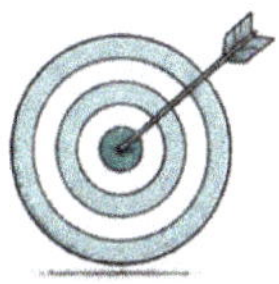

Pick the one that will give you the most relief or impact right now.

3. **COMMIT TO A FIRST STEP**

Define a first step you can take this week. Keep it simple.

4. **GET IT DONE AND BUILD**

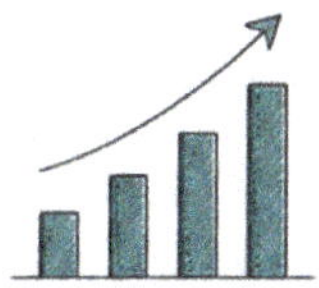

Finish it. Make it a habit. Then pick your next one.

> *Clarity comes from focus.*
> *Momentum comes from finishing.*
> *Growth comes from stacking small wins.*

AI works best when you start small and stay focused. Pick your one thing, get it done, and let that win fuel everything that comes next.

CHAPTER 13

Pick Your One Thing

You've just read seven chapters of things this tool can do.

If you're the kind of person who runs a business, you've been building a list the whole way through. The intake form. The reconciliation. The onboarding process that lives in Marie's head. The explanations you rewrite every April. All of it is worth doing and all of it occurred to you as worth doing.

That list is now the biggest threat to you actually using this.

I've watched this play out enough times to be confident about it. The owner who comes out of a workshop with eleven ideas does less over the following year than the owner who comes out with one. Not slightly less. Dramatically less, and usually nothing at all, because eleven ideas isn't a plan, it's a feeling of possibility, and feelings of possibility evaporate the following Tuesday when a client calls with a real problem.

So this chapter has one job. Get you down to one.

Not your biggest problem

The instinct is to point this at the thing that hurts most. The bottleneck. The process that costs you a weekend every month.

Resist that, at least for now.

Your biggest problem is high stakes by definition, which means you'll be careful with it, which means slow. It probably involves other people, which means coordination. It has resisted solving for years, which usually means it's more tangled than it looks. You'll spend six weeks on it, get a partial result, and quietly conclude this tool is less useful than advertised.

You aren't solving a problem right now. You're building a habit. Those need completely different targets.

Habits are built on things that are frequent, low stakes, and immediately rewarding. Pick accordingly, and get to your biggest problem in month four when using this is automatic.

Three tests

No matrix, no scoring rubric. Three tests, and the answer to all three has to be yes.

One. Do you do it at least once a week?

Frequency is what builds the habit and what compounds the savings. Something you do quarterly saves you four times a year and you'll have forgotten how by the second time. Weekly is the floor. Daily is better.

Two. Would you know immediately if the output were wrong?

This is the Chapter 4 test and it's the safety condition. Pick something where a bad result is obvious on sight and costs you nothing but a redo. That means writing, summarizing, organizing, explaining, drafting. It means not picking anything where being confidently wrong is expensive and hard to spot.

Three. Do you dislike doing it?

This one sounds soft and it isn't. Motivation matters enormously in the first month. A task you resent is a task you'll happily hand over, and you'll notice the relief every single time. A task you're neutral about doesn't generate that feedback, and without the feedback the habit doesn't stick.

If all three are yes, you have your candidate. If you have several, pick the one you dislike most. That's a reasonable tiebreaker.

Worksheet One at the back of this book runs these three tests across five candidates on a single page. Use it if you think in tables. Skip it if you already know your answer.

What good candidates look like

To calibrate, here are the ones I see work most often.

The weekly client update you write for six accounts and resent by the third one. Meeting notes turned into actions and sent within the hour instead of Thursday. Responding to the same five inbound questions you've answered for years. The first draft of any proposal. Cleaning up the export from your system that arrives wrong in the same way every week. Turning your rough voice notes from a site visit into something filed and usable.

Outside an office it looks much the same. A dentist writing the post-op instructions that get handed out twenty times a week. A roofer turning photos and scribbles into an estimate the same evening instead of Sunday night. A shop owner writing the weekly production summary nobody enjoys. A three person law office turning a call into a file note before the next call starts.

Every one of those is weekly or more, obviously right or wrong at a glance, and mildly annoying to do.

And here are the ones that go badly as a first choice. Anything where the answer depends on facts it would have to look up. Anything involving live client financial data before you've sorted out rule two. Anything that requires four other people to change how they work. Anything you do twice a year.

Say it out loud

The last step is to make it specific enough that you'd know whether you did it.

Not "use AI for client communication." That's a category, and categories can't be done.

Write it like this, filling in the blanks:

Every [day or trigger], I will use it to [specific task], which currently takes me about [minutes].

For example:

Every Friday morning, I will use it to draft the weekly update for my six retainer clients, which currently takes me about ninety minutes.

That sentence is your commitment for the next thirty days. It has a trigger, so you don't have to remember. It has a specific task, so you know whether you did it. And it has a number, which Chapter 14 needs.

Write it on the inside cover, under the task you wrote there back in Chapter 1. It's worth seeing how far you've come from that first one.

WHAT TO WATCH FOR

The list isn't wasted, but it needs to leave your head. Everything you thought of while reading Part Two is worth doing eventually. Write it all down somewhere and then close the file. The point isn't to forget it. The point is that it stops competing for attention with the one thing.

One thing feels too small, and that feeling is the trap. You run a business. You're used to moving several things at once and one task feels like a rounding error. It isn't, because you aren't buying the time savings on that one task. You're buying the state of using this fluently, and that only comes from repetition on something narrow.

Don't change your one thing in week two. You'll be tempted, because something better will occur to you around day nine. It always does. Note it, leave it, and finish the thirty days. Switching resets the clock and switching twice is how this ends up abandoned.

DO THIS NOW

Write the sentence. Trigger, task, current minutes.

If you can't fill in the minutes because you've never measured it, guess. A rough number you wrote down beats a precise one you didn't, and Chapter 14 is about to explain why that number matters more than you'd expect.

CHAPTER 14

Give it Thirty Days

Real change takes a little time.
Give yourself thirty days to build momentum and see what's possible.

1 SET YOUR INTENTION

Define what success looks like in thirty days. Be specific.

2 SHOW UP EVERY DAY

Small, consistent actions compound. Progress over perfection.

3 REVIEW AND ADJUST

Check in weekly. What's working? What can you improve?

4 CELEBRATE AND BUILD

Recognize your wins. Then use that momentum to go even further.

> *Thirty days is enough time to create a new habit, see results, and change your business.*

Give AI thirty days of consistent attention, and you'll be amazed at how much you can accomplish—and how far you can take it from there.

CHAPTER 14

Give It Thirty Days

Here's what usually happens without a commitment.

Week one is great. You use it four times, it works, you tell someone about it. Week two you use it twice. Week three there's a deadline and you do the task the old way because the old way is in your hands and you aren't thinking about tools. Week four you don't think about it at all.

Nothing failed. You didn't have a bad experience or decide it was overhyped. The task simply went back to being done the way it has always been done, because that groove is eleven years deep and the new one was four days old.

Thirty days is not a scientific threshold for forming a habit. It is a practical experiment: long enough to create repetition and evidence, short enough to finish. Surviving that month comes down to two things: a number and a trigger.

One number

Pick one measurement. Track it badly. That's the whole system.

The number depends on your task, and any of these work:

- Minutes it used to take, minutes it takes now
- How many you got through
- How long the backlog is
- How many days late you usually are, versus now

For most people it's minutes. If your one thing is the Friday client update at ninety minutes, your number is minutes on Friday.

Track it on paper. Worksheet Two at the back of this book is a thirty day grid built for exactly this. Tear it out and put it on your monitor. If you'd rather not cut up the book, a sticky note with thirty boxes drawn on it does the identical job, and I've seen more of those survive the month than anything printed.

What matters is that it isn't a spreadsheet, isn't an app, and isn't something you have to open. If tracking takes more than four seconds you'll stop by day six and then you'll have no idea whether this worked.

You aren't building a dataset. You're building evidence, for an audience of one, against a specific failure mode. On day 30 you're going to make a decision about whether to keep doing this, and you'll make it based on how you feel about it unless you have something better. Feelings at day 30 are unreliable, because by then the old pain has faded and the new effort is fresh. That's exactly the arithmetic that kills good habits.

Ninety minutes down to twenty five, written on paper in your own handwriting, is very hard to argue with.

A trigger, not a plan

The second thing you need is for the task to start without you deciding to start it.

You already wrote this in Chapter 13. "Every Friday morning." That's a trigger, and it's doing more work than it appears to be.

The reason is that the failure mode isn't motivation, it's memory. You don't skip week three because you decided the tool wasn't worth it. You skip it because Friday arrived, you had a thing to do, and the tool never entered your mind. The old way is automatic and the new way requires a thought, and on a busy Friday the thought doesn't happen.

So attach it to something that happens anyway. Not "when I get around to it." After the Monday meeting. Before I leave on Friday. When the export lands. First thing after lunch.

If you need a calendar reminder for the first two weeks, set one. There's nothing undignified about that. Take it off when you stop needing it.

What the four weeks look like

Knowing the shape in advance makes the middle survivable.

Week one is slower than the old way. Expect this. You're learning how to describe the task and you'll do it badly the first two times. The ninety minute job takes a hundred. This is the week people quit, and they quit having concluded something reasonable from genuinely bad evidence.

Write down the number anyway. You'll want it later.

Week two it gets even. You've worked out how much context to give it and you've stopped starting from scratch each time. Roughly a wash on time, better on quality, and it stops feeling like an experiment.

Week three is where the gap opens. This is usually when people go and set up their standing instructions from Chapter 11, because they're now doing the same task for the fourth time and the repetition is annoying them. Half an hour of setup here pays for the entire month.

Week four it's just how you do the task. You'll notice this on a day you're in a hurry and reach for it without thinking. That's the whole objective, and when it happens you're done.

Day thirty

Look at your tracker and make one of three calls.

Keep it. The number improved and the task is now normal. Nothing to do. Go to Chapter 13, take the second thing off your list, and run another thirty days.

Expand it. The number improved a lot and you can see three adjacent tasks it obviously applies to. Good. Do one of them, not three.

Kill it. The number didn't move, or it moved and you hated the work anyway.

That third option is real and I want to be clear that I mean it. Sometimes the task was a bad choice. Sometimes the output needed so much editing that the savings were fictional. Sometimes you just don't want to work this way, and that's a legitimate finding.

If you kill it, kill the task, not the tool. Go back to Chapter 13, check your candidate against the three tests honestly, and pick a different one. A failed thirty days often traces to a poor first task, and the most common poor choice is something you only do twice a month.

WHAT TO WATCH FOR

Don't tell everyone in week one. The temptation after a good first week is to bring it to the whole team. Wait. You don't yet know where it breaks, and rolling out something you've used four times is how you end up personally supporting a tool you barely understand. Finish your thirty days. Then you have a real answer when someone asks whether it's worth it.

The number will lie to you in one specific way. Time saved on the task doesn't count the time you spent checking the output. Count the checking. A ninety minute job that's now twenty five minutes of drafting plus fifteen of review is forty, not twenty five. Forty is still excellent, and honest numbers are the only ones worth writing down.

Skipping one week is normal and doesn't reset anything. You'll miss a Friday. Something will come up. Pick it back up the next week and don't treat it as failure, because treating it as failure is how a missed week turns into a missed month.

DO THIS NOW

Get your tracker on your monitor, whether that's Worksheet Two or thirty boxes you drew yourself. Not in a drawer.

Write today's date in box one and your current number next to it.

Then set the recurring calendar reminder for your trigger, for the next four weeks only.

That's the whole system, and it'll take you under three minutes.

CHAPTER 15

Ignore Ninety-Five Percent of the Noise

Not every tool. Not every trend. Not every opinion.
Focus on what matters for your business.

1 TUNE OUT THE NOISE

Most of what you hear is designed to distract, not to help. Let it go.

2 FOCUS ON WHAT MOVES THE NEEDLE

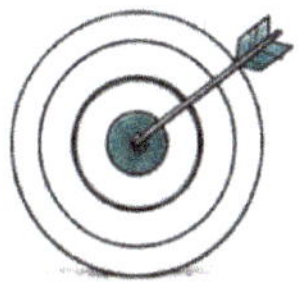

Double down on the few things that create real value for your business and your customers.

3 TRUST YOUR PLAN AND EXECUTE

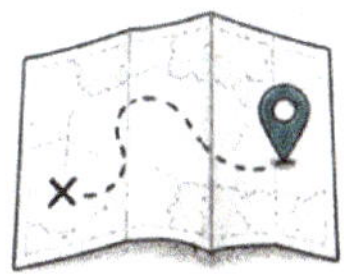

Clear priorities. Consistent action. Better results. That's the real edge.

> *Simplicity isn't about doing less. It's about doing the right less.*

The fastest way to get results with AI is to reject the noise, focus on what matters, and execute with clarity.

CHAPTER 15

Ignore Ninety-Five Percent of the Noise

Somebody in your peer group is going to bring up something at the next meeting that you've never heard of and can't pronounce.

You'll feel briefly behind. That evening you'll read three articles about it and understand roughly a quarter of what you read. Two months later it'll have been replaced by a different thing you've never heard of, and the first thing will have quietly turned out to matter to approximately nobody.

This happens to everyone and it isn't an accident. There's a large industry producing AI news, and its business model requires you to feel like something is happening that you're missing. The volume isn't a signal about how fast the field is moving. It's a signal about how many people are being paid to write about it.

This is the only chapter in this book with a framework in it. The three questions come from The AI Owner's Manual, and they're the thing to write on a sticky note if you take one thing from Part Four.

Where the number comes from

I should be straight with you about the title, because this book has spent fourteen chapters telling you to be suspicious of confident numbers.

Ninety five percent isn't a measurement. Nobody has counted. It's a working ratio, and here's the test that produced it.

Take the AI headlines that will cross your desk this month. For each one, ask whether it names something you could use on a Friday afternoon. Not something impressive. Not something that will matter in five years. Something you could open and use before the weekend.

Do that honestly for a month and you'll land somewhere around one in twenty. Some months two. That's where the number comes from, and it's about as precise as it needs to be, because the decision it drives is binary. You either spend your evenings reading about this or you don't.

The thing that is actually true

Here's what I tell owners who feel behind, and I've been doing this long enough to be confident about it.

Very little that genuinely matters to your business will become unavailable because you waited six months.

The capabilities that matter to a small business arrive slowly, get talked about loudly for a year, and are still there when you get to them. Meanwhile the thing everyone is arguing about this week is mostly of interest to people building AI, not people using it.

Someone who ignored every headline for the last three years and just used the tools well is in a considerably better position than someone who read everything and used nothing. I've met both. It isn't close.

The correct amount of AI news for a business owner is about thirty minutes a month. Everything else is entertainment, and there's nothing wrong with entertainment as long as you know that's what you're consuming.

The 3 Questions

Every vendor pitch, every recommendation from a consultant, every "you need this" post, every tool your nephew swears by. All of it goes through the same three questions before you spend a dollar or an hour.

Worksheet Three at the back is this page in a form you can fill in during the call.

One. What specifically does it do?

Push until you get a sentence with a real task in it.

A good answer: "It reads your incoming invoices and pulls the vendor, amount, due date, and account code into your system, and flags anything it is not sure about."

A bad answer: "It leverages AI to optimize your accounts payable workflow."

The test is whether you could explain it to your bookkeeper in one sentence without using the word AI. If you can't, you haven't been told what it does yet, and the reason is usually that there's less there than the pitch implies.

Two. How will I know it worked?

Before you buy, you should be able to name the number that will change.

A good answer: "Time spent on invoice entry. Most customers are at about a third of what they were within a month."

A bad answer: "You'll feel a lot more on top of things." Or a percentage with no basis, which is the same answer wearing a suit.

If they can't tell you how to measure it, one of two things is true. Either it doesn't produce a measurable result, or it does and they'd rather you didn't check. Both are useful to know.

Three. What happens when it fails?

It will fail sometimes. Everything does. The question is what the failure looks like and who catches it.

A good answer: "It flags anything below a confidence threshold for a person to look at, which runs about fifteen percent, and you get a daily exception report."

A bad answer: "It's 99 percent accurate." That isn't an answer to the question. That's an answer to a different, easier question, and the reason they answered it instead is that the real one is uncomfortable.

The vendors worth buying from answer this one readily, because they've thought about it. The ones who get vague here are telling you something important.

Run it on headlines too

The three questions were built for vendors and they work just as well on news.

You read that some new system achieved something remarkable. Ask what it specifically does. Usually the honest answer is that it performed better on a benchmark test, which is interesting and has no bearing on your Friday.

Ask how you'd know it worked, in your business. Usually there's no answer, because the thing being described isn't something you could use.

Ask what happens when it fails. In a headline, nobody has asked.

Three questions and most of what you read collapses in about ten seconds. That isn't cynicism. Most of it genuinely isn't about you.

Thirty minutes a month

Put it on the calendar. Last Friday of the month, half an hour, same as any other recurring commitment.

Spend it on three things.

Ten minutes: what changed in the tool you actually use. Not the field. The one you pay for. They publish notes on what's new and it's usually a short read. This is the highest value ten minutes of the three by a distance, because these are capabilities you can use this afternoon.

Ten minutes: ask it directly. "What has meaningfully changed for small business users in the last month? Search for it. Skip anything that is only relevant to developers or researchers." You'll get a better filtered summary than most newsletters, and it'll tell you when the honest answer is nothing much.

Ten minutes: your own list. The one from Chapter 13, of everything you thought of and set aside. Read it. Is anything on it now worth being the next thirty day project?

That's the entire practice. Thirty minutes, twelve times a year, and you'll be better informed than most of the people who read about this daily.

WHAT TO WATCH FOR

Peer pressure is the strongest force here. The specific sensation of someone in your group describing something you haven't done is more motivating than any vendor pitch, and it isn't a good reason to do anything. Ask them the three questions. Frequently the honest answer is that they set it up, it was interesting, and they haven't touched it since.

The most useful version of this I've seen was a dentist at a peer table asking a very enthusiastic member what number had changed since he installed the thing. There was a pause, and then he said he'd have to look. Nobody was rude and the subject moved on, and four people at that table saved themselves a demo.

Free trials aren't free. The trial costs nothing and evaluating it costs you a day, plus a day for whoever else you pull in, plus the switching cost if you adopt it and it doesn't stick. Run the three questions before the trial, not during.

"Your competitors are already doing this" is a sales technique. It's designed to bypass the three questions by making the decision about fear instead of fit. When you hear it, that's your cue to slow down rather than speed up.

DO THIS NOW

Find an AI vendor email in your inbox. There is one. There are probably nine.

Run it through the three questions. Write the answers down, even if the answer to all three is that you can't tell from the email.

That's usually the outcome, and it's a complete answer. You're done, and it took a minute and a half.

CHAPTER 16

Where to Go Next

You've got the foundation. Now it's time to keep learning, keep building, and keep leading.

1 KEEP LEARNING

Stay curious.
The more you learn,
the more you can do.
Follow trusted sources,
read, listen, and
keep exploring.

2 KEEP PRACTICING

Use AI every week.
Try new ideas,
test small things,
and keep what works.
Experience builds
confidence.

3 KEEP CONNECTING

Share what you learn.
Ask questions.
Help others.
The right community
will accelerate
your growth.

4 KEEP LEADING

You don't need to be
the expert.
You just need to take
the next step and
help your business
move forward.

The future belongs to those who prepare for it today.
You've started the journey—now keep going.
Your business (and your team) will thank you.

AI isn't a destination. It's a journey of continuous improvement.
Keep moving forward. The best is still ahead.

CHAPTER 16

Where to Go Next

Think back to Chapter 1.

You wrote a task on the inside cover. Something boring you'd done before, chosen specifically so you'd know right away whether the result was any good.

If you've done what this book asked, you've since drafted the letter you were avoiding, read something you'd been ignoring for a month, cleaned up a list, practiced a conversation you were dreading, gotten a process out of someone's head, told your team what's okay in one paragraph, and picked one task to do differently for thirty days.

That isn't a small amount. It's more than most people who have been reading about this for two years have actually done.

This last chapter is about what sits past the edge of this book. Not so you go and do it. So you recognize it when someone describes it to you, and so you know it exists when you eventually need it.

Three things past this book

Plainly, without the vocabulary.

A version that knows your business. You've already met the small version of this. The shelf in Chapter 6, where you loaded documents into one place and got answers that came back with a file name attached.

The step up is the same idea pointed at everything. Not four contracts, but every engagement letter, every piece of past work, every internal document your business has produced since it started. Ask how you handled a similar situation in 2023 and it knows, because it has read the file.

This is the most common next step for a firm your size, and the reason to do the small version first is that it tells you whether you're ready for the big one. If your shelf was quick to assemble because your documents are where they should be, this is a straightforward project. If pulling four contracts together took you an afternoon of hunting through folders and one of them only existed in somebody's email, that's your answer, and the work in front of you is filing rather than AI.

Nobody selling this will mention that part.

Tools that do the work without you starting it. Everything in this book began with you typing. The next step is connecting it to your other software so that things happen on their own. A document arrives, gets read, gets filed, and the right person gets a note about it, with nobody involved.

This is where real hours come out of a business, and it's also where the failures get expensive, because a mistake made once at your keyboard is different from a mistake made four hundred times overnight while you sleep.

Tools that do a whole job. The newest of the three and the one that generates the most breathless coverage. Rather than answering one request, they work through a multi step task on their own, deciding what to do next as they go.

This is real, it's improving quickly, and for a business your size it's mostly not ready. When someone at your next meeting mentions it, the three questions from Chapter 15 are the right response, and question three is the one that matters most.

You don't need any of this yet. Every one of them assumes you already have the habit, and the habit is worth more than all three combined. Come back to this list in a year.

When to go further

Some specific signs you're ready for The AI Owner's Manual rather than another pass through this book.

You've run more than one thirty day project and both stuck. You're being asked by your own team for access rather than the other way around. You're on a licensed or regulated footing and the four rules aren't enough. You're looking at a purchase over a few thousand dollars and want a real evaluation rather than three questions. Or you've hit the thing where it would be genuinely valuable if only it could see your systems, and you've started wondering what that would take.

Any of those and the four rules have become a floor you're standing on rather than a ceiling.

The AI Owner's Manual is the implementation book. It covers the parts this one deliberately leaves out: scoring opportunities, building the business case, the ninety-day rollout model, governance, vendor evaluation, and the three things above in full detail. It is available at jesscoburn.com/book/ and assumes you have already done what you did here.

The workshops are the version where you build it in a room with other owners rather than alone at your desk. Some people work better that way and there's no shame in knowing which you are.

What I would actually tell you

If we were sitting across a table and you asked what to do next, I wouldn't point at any of that.

I'd ask whether you finished the thirty days.

Everything past this book is a multiplier on a habit. If the habit is there, all of it is worth having eventually. If it isn't, none of it helps, and the owner with a sophisticated setup and no habit is in a worse position than the one who just uses it well every Friday, because he has spent money and gotten nothing.

The gap between owners who get a lot out of this and owners who get nothing has almost nothing to do with tools, budget, or technical ability. I've watched a sixty three year old contractor who doesn't own a laptop run circles around firms with a technology committee. He picked one thing, did it every week, and after a year it was ten things because each one had gotten easy enough that adding another cost him nothing.

That's the whole method. It isn't sophisticated and it doesn't photograph well, which is probably why nobody sells it.

The last thing

The reason to do any of this isn't efficiency.

It's that there's a version of your week where the parts you're good at and the parts you enjoy take up more of it, and the parts that are just necessary take up less. Not because you delegated them to a person you have to manage. Because they got smaller.

You've been running your business for a long time and the tedious parts have been the price of admission the whole way. A meaningful share of them no longer has to be.

Start Friday. One thing. Thirty days.

That's it. That's the book.

Jess Coburn jesscoburn.com

BACK OF THE BOOK

Appendix & Worksheets

The tool guide, three worksheets you can fill in, and a glossary of the words you can safely ignore.

APPENDIX

The Tool Guide

A curated list of tools to help you work smarter, save time, and grow your business with AI.

1 WHAT'S INCLUDED
AI assistants, productivity tools, automation platforms, and more.

2 HOW WE EVALUATE
We focus on ease of use, value, security, and how well it actually gets the job done.

3 PRICING AT A GLANCE
Know the cost before you commit—from free options to enterprise plans.

4 BEST FOR BUSINESS OWNERS
Tools chosen specifically for small and mid-sized businesses.

5 TRUST & SECURITY
We only recommend tools we trust with your data and your business.

The right tools won't transform your business. But they will help you transform the way you work.

Use this guide as your starting point.
Test what fits. Build your stack. And keep refining until you have the tools that help you win.

APPENDIX

The Tool Guide

> Everything mentioned was checked in July 2026. It is the only part of this book besides Chapter 2 that names a product, and it is the part most likely to be out of date by the time you read it.
>
> Current version: https://jesscoburn.com/resources/.

Here is how fast this section ages.

While this book was being finished, Google renamed one of the tools on this page. It had been called NotebookLM since it launched. In the middle of July 2026 it became Gemini Notebook. Same website, same product, same notebooks, different name on the door.

That's why the rest of the book doesn't mention a single product by name. A conversation ages slowly. A price list ages in weeks.

So treat these four pages the way you'd treat a printed airline schedule. Useful today, worth checking before you rely on it.

Four categories, not eleven products

The single most useful thing in this appendix isn't the list. It's that most tools relevant to a small business owner's first month fall into one of four operational buckets.

Once you can sort a new tool into a bucket, you can tell in about ten seconds whether it's for you.

One. The box. You type, it answers, you push back. This is what Chapters 1 through 11 are about.

Two. The grounded notebook. You load in your own documents and it answers only from those. Chapter 6, shape four.

Three. The delegate. You hand over a job with several steps and it works through it while you do something else.

Four. The developer version. Same underlying engine, built for people who write software. Probably not you yet.

For the work in this book, that is enough of the landscape to make a good first decision.

Category one: the box

Covered in Chapter 2, so this is the short version.

ChatGPT from OpenAI, Claude from Anthropic, Gemini from Google, and Copilot from Microsoft if you live in Word, Excel, and Outlook.

All four have a usable free tier. All four have a paid personal plan at roughly twenty dollars a month. Pick one on the thirty second rule in Chapter 2 and stop reading comparisons.

What to actually pay attention to: whether it's a business or team plan, not which brand it is. That's rule two in Chapter 12 and it matters more than the choice between them.

Category two: the grounded notebook

Gemini Notebook, from Google. Free at notebooklm.google with any Google account. Called NotebookLM until July 2026.

You create a notebook, upload your documents into it, and ask questions. The distinguishing feature is grounding. It is designed to answer from the files you provide and show you which source supports the answer, rather than relying mainly on general model memory.

For a reader who spent Chapter 4 learning to distrust invented citations, that constraint is the point. It can still misread a source, overstate what it supports, or attach the wrong citation. Verify important claims against the cited passage.

What it costs. The free tier holds 100 notebooks with 50 sources in each and allows 50 questions a day. For a small business that's not a starter portion, that's the whole meal. Paid tiers raise those ceilings and come bundled with Google's AI subscriptions rather than being sold on their own.

Size limits. Each source can run to about 500,000 words or 200 megabytes. There's no page limit. In practice you will not hit this.

Two things that will trip you up. Copy-protected PDFs won't import at all, on any tier, and you'll get an unhelpful error rather than an explanation. And when you paste a web address it pulls the text only, so if the part you need is an image or sits behind a login, save it as a document and upload that instead.

Who it's wrong for. Anyone who wants it to draft, argue, or think alongside them. It's a reference librarian, not a colleague. Keep the box for that.

Category three: the delegate

Cowork, from Anthropic. It isn't a separate purchase. It's a mode inside the Claude desktop application, sitting next to regular chat, and it comes with the paid plan. Check the pricing page before you count on any specific figure, because this is the item on this page most likely to have moved.

The difference from the box is that you hand over a whole job rather than one question. Read through this folder, pull the numbers out, put them in a spreadsheet, and write me a summary. Then it goes and does that while you do something else, showing you each step as it goes.

You give it access folder by folder. It cannot read anything you haven't handed it.

This is the one people often mean when they say Claude Code and get the name wrong. It uses related technology without a terminal and is built for people who do not write software. Anthropic's own usage research shows Cowork is used heavily for nonprogramming work.

Three honest cautions, and I'd rather give you these than a sales pitch.

It burns through your monthly usage far faster than chatting does. A few big jobs can eat a day's allowance.

Multistep work that spans several applications remains unreliable. Simple jobs such as finding and summarizing files are more dependable. Long chains still need close supervision.

And Anthropic itself warns about two specific risks: instructions hidden inside a document it reads, and files being lost or overwritten. Point it at copies, not originals, until you trust it.

Who it's wrong for. Anyone who hasn't finished Chapter 14. This is a multiplier on a habit you don't have yet. It'll still be here in three months and it'll be better.

Category four: the developer version

Claude Code, from Anthropic. Also Codex from OpenAI and similar tools from others.

These run in a terminal window or inside the software developers use to write code. They're for delegating programming work.

I'm naming it for one reason only. Somebody at your next peer group meeting is going to say the words "Claude Code" with real enthusiasm, and you're going to wonder whether you're behind. You aren't. It's a tool for a trade you aren't in.

If you employ developers, forward it to them. Otherwise the answer is Cowork.

What this costs, all in

For a small business owner following this book:

What	Roughly
One box, personal plan	About $20 a month; data and admin settings vary
One box, business or team plan	About $20 to $30 per seat; minimum commitment varies
Grounded notebook	Free is genuinely enough
Delegate	Included with the paid box plan
Developer version	Not applicable

For one owner, the practical total ranges from about twenty dollars for a personal plan to the provider's minimum business commitment. Do not look only at the seat price. Check minimum seats, required base subscriptions, data terms, and administrative control. Rule two in Chapter 12 exists for a reason.

WHAT TO WATCH FOR

The categories are stable. The names are not. In the eighteen months before this was written, one of these products was renamed, one was launched, and one changed price twice. The four buckets did not move. Learn the buckets.

Bundled is not free. Several of these arrive included with something you already pay for, which is convenient and also how you end up with four subscriptions doing the same job. Before you add anything, check what you already have.

The major chat tools in category one have free tiers, but lower limits can make them a poor first impression. Chapter 2 explains what to compare before you choose.

Check the address bar. There are convincing fake versions of every product named here, and the paid search results above the real one are not always the real one. Type the address.

Prices, plan names, and product names checked July 2026. The maintained resource page is refreshed quarterly at http://jesscoburn.com/resources/. If something here does not match what you see on the screen, the screen is right.

WORKSHEET ONE

Your One Thing

From Chapter 13. Fill this in before you start your thirty days.

Step one. Five tasks you thought of while reading Part Two.

Step two. Run the three tests. All three have to be yes.

	Weekly or more?	Would I know if it were wrong?	Do I dislike it?
1			
2			
3			
4			
5			

If more than one scores three out of three, pick the one you dislike most.

Step three. Write the sentence.

Every ________________________,

I will use it to ________________________________,

which currently takes me about ______ minutes.

Step four. Everything else goes here, and then you close this page.

Come back to this list on the last Friday of the month, per Chapter 15.

WORKSHEET TWO

The Thirty Day Tracker

From Chapter 14. Print this and put it on your monitor. Not in a drawer.

My one thing ______________________________

My trigger ______________________________

Starting number ______________________________

What I am measuring (circle one): minutes · how many · backlog · days late · other ______

1	2	3	4	5	6
7	8	9	10	11	12
13	14	15	16	17	18
19	20	21	22	23	24
25	26	27	28	29	30

What to expect, so the middle doesn't throw you

- Week one is slower than the old way. Write the number down anyway.
- Week two is roughly even on time, better on quality.
- Week three is where the gap opens. Go set up your standing instructions.
- Week four it's just how you do the task.

Count your checking time. A ninety minute job that's now twenty five minutes of drafting plus fifteen of review is forty, not twenty five.

Day thirty. Circle one.

KEEP IT. The number improved and the task is normal now. Go pick the next one.

EXPAND IT. Do one adjacent task, not three.

KILL IT. Kill the task, not the tool. Go back to Worksheet One and pick again.

Ending number ________ Change ________

WORKSHEET THREE

The 3 Questions

From Chapter 15. Every vendor pitch, every recommendation, every headline. Before you spend a dollar or an hour.

What is being pitched ______________________________

1. What specifically does it do?

Push until you get a sentence with a real task in it. Test: could you explain it to your bookkeeper in one sentence without using the word AI?

☐ Got a real answer ☐ Not yet

2. How will I know it worked?

Name the number that will change. If they cannot tell you how to measure it, either it does not produce a measurable result or they would rather you did not check.

☐ Got a real answer ☐ Not yet

3. What happens when it fails?

What does the failure look like, who catches it, and how do you recover? "It is 99 percent accurate" is not an answer to this question.

☐ Got a real answer ☐ Not yet

Three real answers? Worth a closer look. Any deflection? You have your answer, and it took under two minutes.

TWO PHRASES THAT MEAN SLOW DOWN

"Your competitors are already doing this." · "This offer is only available through the end of the month."

Glossary

Plain English. If a term is not here, you did not need it.

Agent. A tool that works through a multi step job on its own, deciding what to do next as it goes, rather than answering one request at a time. Real, improving fast, mostly not ready for a small business. See Chapter 16.

AGI. Artificial general intelligence. A hypothetical future system that can do essentially any intellectual task a person can. Nobody agrees on the definition or the date. If it comes up at your peer group meeting, nothing about your Friday changes.

API. A way for two pieces of software to talk to each other without a person in between. You will hear it when someone describes connecting this to your other systems. It is a plumbing word, not a product.

Automation. Connecting it to your other software so things happen without you starting them. A document arrives, gets read, gets filed, someone gets a note. This is where real hours come out of a business and also where mistakes get repeated at scale.

Chatbot. Any tool you talk to in a box. Includes everything in this book and also the thing on your bank's website that cannot help you. The word covers too much to be useful.

Cutoff date. The date after which a model's built-in training knowledge may be incomplete. Some tools can search current sources, but confirm that search is active and check the cited source. See Chapter 4.

Custom instructions. The settings page where you write things you want applied to every conversation. Sometimes called preferences or personalization. The single most underused feature in any of these tools. See Chapter 11.

Free tier. The version that costs nothing. Usable, but it usually has lower limits and less access to higher-capability models and tools. Data use depends on the provider and your settings. See Chapters 2 and 12.

GPT. Generative pre-trained transformer. The technical name for the design most of these are built on. It ended up in one company's product name, which is why people use it as though it means the whole category. It does not.

Hallucination. The industry's word for when it makes something up. A bad word, because it suggests something rare and exotic. It is neither. It is the machine doing what it always does, in a case where the plausible answer and the true one came apart. See Chapter 4.

Large language model (LLM). The full name for the thing this book calls a very good guesser. Usually shortened to three letters. When someone says it, they mean the engine inside the box you type into.

Model. The thing underneath the app. When people talk about a new model, they mean the engine got replaced. You will notice the app looks the same and the answers get better.

Prompt. What you type. That is all it means. The industry has produced an enormous amount of writing about prompt engineering, and for the work in this book it reduces to: say what you want, give it the context, tell it what you did not like, ask again.

Retrieval. Any setup where it answers from a specific set of documents rather than from general memory. This is the "version that knows your business" in Chapter 16. You will hear it called by a three letter abbreviation that is not worth learning.

Token. How these tools count the text going in and out, for pricing purposes. Roughly three quarters of a word. You will see it on pricing pages and you can safely ignore it.

Training data. Information used to build or improve a model. Whether your conversations may be used for improvement depends on the service, plan, and settings. Business workspaces generally provide stronger default terms. See Chapter 12.

NOTES

Notes & Sources

This book is designed to be practical rather than academic. These are the principal notes behind its named case, current product claims, and examples.

Examples

The examples are illustrative. Where they draw on real situations, identifying details and figures have been changed.

Current product information

Product names, plan prices, limits, and privacy terms were checked against official vendor pages in July 2026. They change quickly. The maintained links and quarterly updates are at https://jesscoburn.com/resources/. Thirty days is used as a practical experiment, not as a universal claim about how long habit formation takes.

Principal sources

Mata v. Avianca, Inc., No. 22-cv-1461 (S.D.N.Y.), sanctions order filed June 22, 2023.

Google, "NotebookLM is now Gemini Notebook," July 16, 2026; Gemini Notebook Help, "Frequently asked questions."

OpenAI, "Business Data Privacy, Security, and Compliance"; ChatGPT Business plan and billing documentation.

Anthropic, Claude Cowork product documentation; Claude plan and Team billing documentation; Anthropic Economic Index.

Microsoft and Google official Microsoft 365 Copilot, Workspace, Gemini, and Google AI plan documentation.

Start Friday. One thing. Thirty days.

That's it. That's the book.

ABOUT THE AUTHOR

Jess Coburn

Jess Coburn works with owners of small and mid-sized businesses on getting practical value out of AI — in their own offices, on their own work, without a technology committee.

The AI On-Ramp is the starting book. The AI Owner's Manual is the next-stage implementation guide: scoring opportunities, building the business case, the ninety-day rollout model, governance, and vendor evaluation. The workshops are the version where you build it in a room with other owners rather than alone at your desk.

Companion resources and quarterly updates: https://jesscoburn.com/resources/

www.ingramcontent.com/pod-product-compliance
Lightning Source LLC
LaVergne TN
LVHW022227200926
848481LV00006B/2150